A RAILWAY MODELLER'S PICTURE LIBRARY

A RAILWAY MODELLER'S PICTURE LIBRARY

CHRIS LEIGH

BCA
LONDON NEWYORK SYDNEY TORONTO

Contents

This edition published 1995 by BCA
by arrangement with Ian Allan Publishing
an imprint of Ian Allan Ltd,
Terminal House, Station Approach,
Shepperton, Surrey TW17 8AS

CN3218

Printed by Ian Allan Printing Ltd,
Coombelands House, Coombelands Lane,
Addlestone, Surrey KT15 1HY.

Front cover:
Top left: Shepperton station, 1991.
Bottom left; Hazelend bridge, Calne.
Centre top: Interior of manual signalbox.
Centre bottom left: Leominster engine shed, 1959. *Colour-Rail*
Centre bottom right: Ketton signalbox.
Top right: Gunnislake station. *K. A. Jaggers*
Bottom right: (G)WR lower quadrant semaphore.

Back cover:
Top left: Holyhead station. *K. A. Jaggers*
Centre left: Mortimer station.
Bottom left: Lower quadrant junction signal, Castle Cary. *Nick Lerwill*
Top right: Hagley station.
Centre right: Modern BR station. *BR*
Bottom right: GWR cattle-creep bridge, Hungerford.

All cover photographs by the author unless otherwise indicated.

Half-title page: A view of Little Somerton station. *Real Photographs*

Title page:
Oundle station, Northamptonshire, was completed in 1845 to the design of John Livock and stands today as a private house. Oundle and Wansford are the last surviving examples of his elegant railway work in local stone under a Collyweston slate roof. The platform canopy, no longer extant at either station, is carried on decorative iron brackets with no supporting columns and no decorative valancing. The platforms at Oundle were staggered, the photographer of this 19th century view standing with his back to the platform for northbound trains on the Northampton–Peterborough line.
Author's collection

Introduction

WHENEVER I begin a modelling project, the first thing I do is to go looking for photographs. It really doesn't matter whether I am planning to add details to a ready-to-run locomotive model, or setting out to build a complete layout or diorama, the need for photographs is the same. It is true, too, that the need for reference photographs is the same whether it's to check details on a locomotive or to model a non-railway item such as a building or a section of scenery.

Equally, study of photographs sometimes prompts a model. On a recent visit to a local village for a Sunday afternoon walk, I found a glorious stone-built watermill with an adjacent ford, now used only by an occasional tractor. I took lots of photographs in readiness for the model which I might build one day.

Where railway photographic research is concerned, I relied for years on the extensive Ian Allan Library. As an editor I had unrestricted access and could consult all the photographs I needed, even if it was just for my own curiosity. However, since leaving Ian Allan Ltd I have come to realise just how much I used that facility for my modelling research. Suddenly, my research facilities now consist only of my own photographs and small collection of books.

Now I appreciate how difficult it is for the reader when modelling magazine articles glibly suggest that the modeller 'should consult photographs' for further details. This book is designed to address that problem, at least as far as is possible in one volume.

The brief was to provide reference photographs for a wide range of fixed railway equipment — everything, that is, except locomotives and rolling stock. It thus takes in everything from station buildings to water columns, from luggage barrows to coaling towers. With such an enormous range, clearly the coverage can by no means be exhaustive, but I have endeavoured to illustrate typical examples from major railway companies and from British Railways and the current, 'post-privatisation', era.

In more recent years and certainly since Nationalisation in 1948, many features of the railway and items of railway equipment have been standardised regardless of their geographical location. The automatic half-barrier crossing, for instance, is pretty much a standard affair whether it be in Scotland or Cornwall. However, if we go back to traditional gated level crossings, many of which date from before the 1923 Grouping, these show considerable variety, although thereafter a degree of standardisation occurred. In general this standardisation related to the 'Big Four' companies created by the Grouping and thus a Great Western Railway level crossing gate was markedly different from, say, a Southern Railway or LMS example.

I have endeavoured, through the captions, to draw attention to such differences and to indicate features which were the same regardless of the railway company which built them. In some subject areas I have chosen to illustrate items which I believe will have particular appeal to model-makers. Thus, there is more concentration on smaller, more 'modelable' stations rather than the Clapham Junctions or Liverpool Lime Streets. Similarly, the sections on bridges concentrate on small structures rather than Saltash or the Forth Bridge. In cases where I know that a particular item is available commercially in model form, I have included relevant information.

Though colour schemes will receive some mention, in general, matters such as liveries and small details such as uniforms and items which can only be modelled in a very large scale have been fully covered elsewhere, and are therefore not included.

The contents are arranged in alphabetical order, and cross-referenced where necessary. In many instances the photographs have been chosen because they contain a wealth of detail as well as the specific subject, so they are worthy of close study.

Chris Leigh
Oundle, Northamptonshire

ARCHES

FROM their earliest days railways have had hundreds of bridges, many of them brick or stone arch structures whose arches have provided useful dry accommodation for all sorts of storage and industrial uses. By the 20th century the letting of bridge arches for private use was commonplace and in the BR period there have actually been concerted efforts to market arches. They can be found as stores, workshops, cafés and retail premises and even the advent of ever more restrictive health and safety regulations does not seem to have affected them.

Above:
Traditional arch conversions such as these with frontages of corrugated iron and transparent corrugated plastic provided useful income for the railway. This brick viaduct at Worcester provides ample headroom for a motor vehicle workshop including a hydraulic inspection lift. *R. M. Clayton*

Above:
The left-hand arch here has a modern brick frontage with folding door, but others are open and merely used for storing contractors' plant. This scene was in Liverpool, before the refurbishing of the arches. *BR*

Below:
An example of modern (mid-1980s) development in which a seedy area has been transformed. The arches below Windsor & Eton Central station form part of a small shopping development linking the riverfront area to the main shopping street. Note that a standard style of shop front has been used to give a neat and uniform appearance. *BR*

ASH DISPOSAL

THE disposal of ash from smokebox cleaning and dropped fires was an essential activity of steam locomotive sheds, large and small. The one essential feature was a pit between the running rails, over which the locomotive could be placed for access when raking out the fire, and into which the ash would drop. The pit would be either brick- or concrete-lined, since it had to be fireproof.

In its simplest form, the ash would be dug laboriously from the pit and loaded into open wagons for disposal. Later, more sophisticated ash disposal systems were evolved for larger locomotive depots. These systems would involve conveyor belts and hopper loading bins for filling the wagons.

Left:
'Britannia' 4-6-2 No 70054 *Dornoch Firth* receives attention at Carlisle Kingmoor depot on 9 August 1966. A large amount of ash has been raked out of the smokebox on to the front platform and it appears that the long dart (poker) leaning on the left buffer has been used to clear blocked tubes. Ash is heaped all around and the further of the two tubs has been filled. *J. L. McIvor*

Above:
At this northeastern depot ash disposal is at least partially mechanised. The pit here contains small wheeled tubs into which the ash is dropped. These are then pushed by hand to a disposal point where they can be tipped on to a conveyor belt loading system.
L. A. Nixon

Right:
The 50-ton-capacity ash bunker at Polmadie depot was photographed for BR in August 1948. The hopper is seen here with a wagon positioned underneath, ready for loading. The conveyor belt is seen to the rear of the bunker in this view. *BR*

BALLAST BINS

USUALLY made of old sleepers or heavy timbers, and later of precast concrete, ballast bins are still a feature of the railway scene, being provided to enable permanent way staff to hand-pack ballast on stretches of track where it is frequently displaced by movement or by an unstable substratum beneath the track.

BARROW CROSSINGS

AT one or both ends of most stations (with more than one platform) a crossing would be provided to enable luggage barrows to be taken across the line safely. At some rural stations where there was no footbridge this crossing might also be used by passengers. The crossing would be made of stout timbers laid parallel to the rails and with appropriate flangeways.

Above:
A two-coach formation of Derby Lightweight vehicles enters Potton with the 12.15pm Bletchley–Cambridge on 16 April 1966. In the foreground is the timber-built barrow crossing joining the ends of the platforms. Note the wedge-shaped timber on the approach side of the ramp in the left-hand track. This was to deflect any low-hanging couplings or other equipment which might hit the crossing. *D. L. Percival*

BICYCLE SHEDS

ALL sorts of sheds have been — and are — used by the railway for cycle storage at stations. Usually of timber or corrugated iron construction, the cycle shed provided safe and inexpensive storage for passengers to leave their cycles out of the rain — the GWR used its corrugated 'pagoda' sheds quite often (see under **Halts** and **Waiting Shelters**). Sometimes a room in the main station building was used for cycle storage — an outside door and some metal cycle racks were all that were needed.

Above:
A cycle store of almost timeless design at Oulton Broad North in 1994. Simple timber framing supports a roof and rear wall of corrugated iron. The cycle racks are the modern concrete slab variety. *Author*

Right:
A corrugated GWR 'pagoda' shed at Fairford. *M. S. Cross*

BOOKSTALLS

THE timber-built bookstall selling newspapers and magazines was a traditional feature of larger stations from the Victorian era. The distinctive pattern with rounded ends beloved of plastic kit manufacturers dates from the 1920s — a splendid example from London Waterloo is preserved at Sheringham, Norfolk.

Above:
Modern stations usually have bookstalls and other retail premises built into the permanent buildings as shown here by this John Menzies shop in the ticket hall of Cardiff Queen Street station dating from 1974. *BR*

BRIDGES (Metal)

WROUGHT iron, and later, steel, were widely used by railway builders for the construction of bridges both under and over the line. The riveted steel span makes for a simple model which is easy to build and, provided that attention is paid to detail, looks good. The accompanying illustrations provide some examples, but see also the sections headed **Bridges (Over Rails)** and **Bridges (Under Rails).**

Right:
Here is a good small plate-girder bridge which carried the Hitchin–Bedford line of the Midland Railway over a minor road. Most such spans were removed when the railway over them closed but this one still existed in 1994. As can be seen, some half-dozen 'I' section girders span the road and are supported on brick piers. Plate girders are also used to form the parapet wall in this instance. The height restriction triangle is a modern addition. *Author*

Below:
LBSCR 'K' class 2-6-0 No 32352 heads the 3.28pm Haywards Heath–London Bridge over Cooks Pond Bridge, an elaborate and substantial lattice-girder construction. The track is carried on top of the girders and the deck of the bridge is timber. Note the decorated brick piers and the lattice parapet.
S. C. Nash/Ian Allan Library

Above:
A much older style of riveted steel through-truss is represented by the swing bridge section of the Barmouth Viaduct, a structure which comprises a long timber trestle with the swing section at its northern end. It is here seen with Ivatt '2MT' 2-6-0 No 46521 crossing with a southbound freight working on 25 July 1963. The two main spans are assembled from lattice-girder sections within a heavy plate frame. A separate walkway is carried on the outside of the main span. A number of crossbeams link the two main spans, above the train, and the whole structure pivots so that it can be turned to allow tall ships to pass. Note that the track in the foreground, on the timber-trestle viaduct section of the structure, is laid on longitudinal timber baulks which also carry a second rail section laid on its side and slightly higher than the running rails. This acts as a check rail to keep any derailed wheels from running outside the track structure, so reducing the risk of a derailed train damaging the bridge structure or toppling off the bridge. *Brian Stephenson*

Below:
A view which demonstrates the enormous space which would be required for a model of Brunel's Royal Albert Bridge, Saltash, in all but the smallest of modelling scales. A nine-coach westbound express is swallowed by the structure in this view from the Devon shore in the 1950s. In this structure the suspension bridge is strengthened by the 'arch' of a hollow wrought-iron tube which assists the suspension chain in carrying the weight of the single-track bridge deck. The two spans are supported on a wrought-iron pier founded on rock in mid-stream. Both ends of the structure are approached over a series of wrought-iron spans on masonry piers. In the foreground is the Torpoint vehicle ferry which, until the construction of the road bridge, was the only means for road traffic to cross the Tamar at this point. *B. A. Butt*

Above:
Many lattice-girder bridges were built as through-trusses where the track is carried through the structure on a series of crossbeams mounted on the two main trusses. Feeder Road Bridge, Bristol, seen here in the mid-1960s, has two bowstring main trusses carried on stone piers, the whole structure being a skew span crossing the waterway at an angle. A plain plate-girder structure spans the adjacent road. *BR*

Left:
A more conventional shape than the bowstring is this through-truss bridge over the River Cynon at Cwmbach in South Wales. Despite its apparent newness this is a refurbished secondhand structure, one of two which carried the Oxford–Princes Risborough line over the A40 trunk road in Oxfordshire. *BR*

Left:
The Severn Railway Bridge, which carried the former Midland Railway single track over the Severn between Sharpness and Lydney, comprised a series of bowstring spans (the largest of which was 327ft long) to make up its 4,161ft total length. The spans were of wrought iron with lattice-girder framing and just two small crossbeams at the apex of each span. One large span, above the Berkeley Ship Canal, was pivoted atop a central stone pier to allow the passage of large ships on the canal. The operating control room was mounted in a signalbox-like structure above this span.

The Severn Bridge was severely damaged by a runaway barge in 1960, two spans being destroyed. It was not repaired and was dismantled some years later. This view shows the swing bridge signalbox from track level, looking towards Lydney.
M. Windeatt/R&TPS

Centre left:
The swing bridge section seen from the bank of the Ship Canal. *Colin Maggs*

Below:
A view through the fixed spans looking towards Lydney.
M. Windeatt/R&TPS

Above:
A view from the Cornish shore of Brunel 's Royal Albert Bridge in 1939 clearly shows the composite nature of the two main spans. The bridge was completed in 1859 shortly before its designer's death at the age of 53. *GWR*

Right:
Where circumstances prevent the installation of a ready-made span, the cantilever system is employed. Here, the structure is designed so that it can be built outwards from both shores to meet in the centre, either by balancing the two sides (as in the Forth bridge) or by tying down the shore ends to counteract the weight of the span, as here at the Connel Ferry Bridge in Scotland. This structure should be of particular interest to modellers as it is a rare example of a British bridge which carried both road and railway. It was completed in 1903 to carry the Ballachulish branch over Loch Etive, and when the branch closed to passengers in 1966 it became a road-only bridge. *Ian Allan Library*

Right:
Caledonian Railway '2P' 0-4-4T No 55124 comes off the Connel Ferry Bridge with the 4.55pm Oban–Ballachulish on 15 May 1961. In the foreground is the narrow roadway, access to which was controlled by a special road and rail signalbox at the far end of the structure, since road traffic could not be permitted on the structure at the same time as trains, due to the restricted width. A complex toll system was also operated for farm animals and road traffic using the bridge and this lasted until after Nationalisation in 1948. *M. Mensing*

Left:
A pair of wrought-iron columns set in the river-bed support the ends of two through-truss girders carrying the Southern Railway line over Little Petherick Creek at Padstow. *Ian Allan Library*

Below:
The vast bulk of the Forth Bridge is evident in this view of the structure in which three balanced cantilevers are used, the balanced structures carrying the weight of the small spans which link them. This mild-steel structure is over 8,000ft long and 360ft high.
Locomotive Publishing Co

BRIDGES (Over Rails)

BRIDGE architecture is a vital feature of almost any model railway and the type and style of bridge and its building materials can determine the geographical setting of the layout. Most bridges over railways carry roads of some sort, though these will vary from country lanes to motorways. There are, too, hundreds of 'accommodation' bridges which allow farmers a route over the railway. They are often not public rights of way and usually carry an unsurfaced farm track wide enough to admit farm machinery. Bridges which carry canals or other watercourses over railways (aqueducts) are less common but they range from the narrow channels, little more than an open-topped pipe, which carried water over the Lynton & Barnstaple Railway to multi-arched stone viaducts too large for the average model railway layout (see also **Footbridges**).

Above:
A simple concrete accommodation bridge which carried a farm track over the Dereham–Fakenham line in Norfolk. Though a straightforward design to model, concrete is a difficult material to represent convincingly in model form. Track is to be relaid through this section from County School station. *Author*

Right:
Most over-line bridges carried roads and the modeller needs to pay just as much attention to this aspect of his model as to the structure below. The amount of growth on these verges almost hides the parapet walls of a simple brick arch bridge over the former London & North Western Railway between Thorpe and Barnwell. *Author*

Above:
A simple steel-girder accommodation bridge with approach ramps to facilitate its use by cattle and sheep. Steel girders support one end but the original stone pier survives at the other end. This sort of bridge could be found over railway lines, though this example crosses the River Nene near Wadenhoe. *Author*

Centre left:
A triple-arch stone bridge which carries the road on a rising gradient, over the railway at Umberleigh, Devon. Note the bridge number on a post in front of the right-hand pier. Bridges were numbered in order to aid identification. A 60mph speed restriction is signposted for the left-hand line, and 'Battle of Britain' No 34066 *Spitfire* is approaching on an Ilfracombe–Salisbury stopping service. *Ian Allan Library*

Left:
This over-line bridge at St Keyne on the Looe branch carries a minor road over the railway and its predecessor, the adjacent canal. The round arch over the canal is original, the bridge having been extended when the railway was built. Steel girders span the single line and carry the stone parapet walls. *Ian Allan Library*

Right:
A very attractive stone arch spans the single line just outside Lugton. The low parapet is topped with short posts carrying wires to prevent the foolhardy from climbing on to the parapet. The 4pm service to Beith is formed by AC Cars diesel railbus No Sc79979. *J. Brown*

Centre right:
Lots of detail for modellers in this view of a stone bridge built by the Ayrshire & Galloway Railway over the line at Minnevey. The bridge frames BR Standard 2-6-0 No 77017 with a Dalmellington–Kilmarnock train on 28 March 1959. The construction of a stone elliptical arch is well illustrated. *G. H. Robin*

Below:
The other end of the bridge architect's spectrum is illustrated by these spans which are so well known that they readily identify this view as Sonning cutting. The nearer bridge is a wrought-iron span carried on brick piers. Whatever the motive power passing beneath it, the style of this bridge seems to celebrate the subject, providing a perfect frame. *BR*

Above:
At Buckley on the Wrexham, Mold & Connah's Quay line stood this rather crude stone arch, photographed in 1948. The arch is founded on five courses of bricks with stonework above and the workmanship seems a little 'rustic'. *LGRP*

Below:
A steel-girder accommodation bridge over the GWR line at Staines West. This bridge is one of three, joined end to end, which allow access to grazing on Staines Moor at a point where the GWR, Wyrardisbury River and LSWR lines run side by side. A pair of yellow brick arches span the river and a single red brick arch spans the SR lines. *Author*

BRIDGES (Swing)

BRIDGES over navigable waterways are required to have sufficient clearance to permit vessels of a specified height to pass underneath. Where the railway crosses such a waterway with insufficient clearance (for example in very flat terrain such as in parts of Norfolk and Suffolk) at least one span of the bridge will be made to move. In Europe, lifting bridges are widely used, but in the UK the swing bridge is more usual. Railway swing bridges are nowadays quite unusual but a number do still survive. Notable examples include Banavie, where the West Highland line crosses the Caledonian Canal, and Barmouth.

Above and right:
Two views of Oulton Broad swing bridge in Suffolk, where the Ipswich–Lowestoft line crosses Oulton Broad. The bridge is now single track and carries only a limited passenger service of around a dozen trains per day. In its heyday it would have carried extensive freight traffic from Lowestoft. The long plate-girder span which pivots is supported by truss-rods from a girder frame mounted above the central pier on which the structure turns. To judge from the number of tall vessels above the bridge it must see frequent use during the summer. It is controlled from a Great Eastern Railway timber signalbox situated on the north bank of the Broad (see **Signalboxes [Manual]**). *Author*

BRIDGES (Under Rails)

HERE we encounter an even wider variety, for railways cross thousands of watercourses, from drainage ditches to river estuaries, as well as all sizes and types of road, and even other railways. The under-line accommodation bridge was possibly even more common than the over-line type, these being necessary to permit farm animals free movement between fields on property which had been bisected by the railway line.

The nature of railway construction enabled many under-line bridges to be constructed of iron or steel — materials which are still used today for such work although many modern bridges employ concrete beams. Early railway engineers paid great attention to the styling of their bridges, particularly those built in stone, and some very fine examples, both large and small, still exist.

Above:
A comparatively simple model to build would be this plate-girder design with three curved-top steel spans. The model could be built using styrene sheet or even a soldered brass construction. Note that the spans are staggered to suit the angle at which the river is crossed, the ends of the girders resting on offset pairs of cylindrical piers in mid-stream. A train to Aberystwyth is crossing the River Towy near Carmarthen on 20 June 1951. *J. N. Westwood*

Above:
A mixture of curved-top and straight plate-girder spans is evident in this view on an inlet of the Thames at Bourne End. The underside of this bridge is only a few feet above the water (which was quite low at the time) and the spans are supported on brick piers. Note the handrails provided on the straight span, the girders of which come just to solebar height on the DMU. *Author*

Centre right and below right:
Two views of an under-line bridge suitable for the modern-image modeller, having been installed in 1980. The modern welded steel girders are carried on plain concrete abutments, the structure carrying a siding over the Wyrardisbury River at Staines. Note the mounting arrangement under the far end of the main girder. The view from track level on the same bridge shows the very plain nature of the girders, the box-section handrails and, on the right, the concrete steps which provide a walkway over the top of the girders. The walkway is surfaced with a black non-slip material and the track is reclaimed bullhead panels (dating from pre-Nationalisation) on a ballast base. *Author*

Left and centre left:
For comparison, two views of a much earlier and smaller culvert over a stream at Poyle on the West Drayton–Staines branch. Here, riveted steel girders are carried on brick abutments. The handrails are of 'L' section material and a narrow timber walkway is set outside the girders. Normal ballasted track is carried on the steel deck of the structure. *Author*

Below:
A cattle-creep or under-line accommodation bridge built of yellow bricks and providing a perfect prototype for modelling. Brick wing walls capped with engineering 'blues' retain the sides of the embankment while the arch itself is well proportioned. A '14XX' 0-4-2T is seen near Yeoveney Halt, heading for Staines West in the 1950s. Though the railway has gone, this bridge still survives, close by the M25 motorway!
D. Sutton/Ian Allan Library

Above:
A more recent close-up of the cattle-creep near Yeoveney Halt shows clearly the straight sides to the arch, which is formed of three courses of bricks — of which the ends are seen. The wing walls are concealed by vegetation in this 1980s view. *Author*

Centre right
This skew-span steel-girder bridge carried the GWR line over the SR at Staines and was built for double-track although only a single line was ever laid. Three riveted plate-steel girders are carried on brick piers, the ballasted track being carried by the two girders nearest the camera. The steel bridge deck on the unused side was left exposed. The steelwork in the foreground is the remains of Staines Moor signalbox, destroyed by fire. *Author*

Below right:
A typical GWR plate-girder structure carries the main line over the River Teign at Newton Abbot, seen here on 6 March 1961. The height of the girder on the right has been increased by adding to the top. In the BR era such structures were generally painted dark grey or black. *Ian Allan Library*

Right:
Four views of Brunel's splendid Royal Albert Bridge over the Tamar at Saltash. First, a 1937 view looking upstream with the Devon bank on the right. The suspension chains are strengthened and stiffened by the oval-section wrought-iron tubes. The centre pile is sunk on a rock in mid-stream. *GWR*

Below:
The view from the Devon bank reveals that the structure is single track, approached by seven plate-girder spans. Single-line token working was employed over the bridge — the 'engine sandwich' auto-train working was common on Saltash–Plymouth local services. *B. A. Butt*

Above:
A 'Grange' class 4-6-0 heads across the bridge with a train from Penzance in 1954. *Donald Kelk*

Below:
A close-up of the stone pier and plate-girder approach during maintenance work in 1964 clearly shows the crossbeams and timber decking of the approach span. *G. M. Cashmore*

Top:
Described by the Western Region in 1974 as 'speedy bridge construction' this modern concrete span near Shrivenham is carried on steel-faced abutments set in a concrete plinth at road level, the concrete being more resistant to damage. Note how the abutments are shaped to retain the embankment. *BR*

Above:
In connection with the widening of the Shenfield line to increase the number of tracks, an interesting structure has been created here, with a newer steel span placed alongside a much older brick arch. In view of the obvious hazard to road traffic presented by the very low arch, one suspects that this was subsequently replaced with a matching plate-steel span. *BR*

Above:
Spidery lattice-girder viaducts make for attractive if complex models. This example on the West Highland line is carried on slender stone piers. The deck would be cross-timbered and there is a metal safety fence along each side. *BR*

Below:
Four-and-a-half plate-girder spans provide the approach to the substantial lattice span over the River Nene at Wansford. The spans are carried on stone piers and have 'I' section brackets carrying a walkway riveted to the sides. Steel posts support a three-rung handrail. Steps, more recently installed, give access from a riverside footpath to the road level on the other side of the river. No 60103 *Flying Scotsman* crosses in July 1994. *Author*

BUFFER STOPS

BUFFER stops, or stop blocks, installed to prevent stock running off the end of sidings, were of a very distinctive design, usually related to the railway which built them. Though hydraulic buffers could be found at some major termini, most stop blocks were much more homespun, usually being built from rail and sleepers but to a standard pattern.

Below:
A Great Central example at Barton-on-Humber is similar to, but more substantial than, the GER type opposite below. Bolted plates hold the vertical rails and the main supports are at a shallower angle. A much deeper cast bracket holds three sections of bullhead rail. For safe use at night an oil lamp is provided on a stout timber post, complete with access ladder. *Brian Morrison*

Right:
The GWR pattern employed bullhead rails bent to shape and fish-bolted to the track. Three vertical pieces of rail either side provided further support and a means of attachment for the timber sleeper. On this example an old sleeper has been used and its chair-fixing holes can be clearly seen. The stop-block rails were painted black, often with the front face of the sleeper painted red. Where necessary an oil lamp would be mounted on the centre of the beam. *Author*

Right:
A view showing the rear of a similar structure at Fairford. *M. Cross*

Centre right:
The GWR design adapted by BR Western Region provides a short checkrail section where the stop-block rails are extended for three sleepers span, inside the running rails. Instead of an old sleeper, four lengths of rail have been employed, with additional short lengths placed where the wagon buffers would make contact. The rails were painted white but quickly weathered to rust red. *Author*

Below:
Quite a different pattern is represented by this Great Eastern Railway example surviving, albeit rather derelict, in 1994. Three vertical sections of bullhead rail are held together at the top by a metal band. The main bullhead rail sections are bent in a curve and bolted to the verticals. Special cast brackets hold the remains of a rotted timber sleeper. The fixings to the track are deeply covered by ballast and debris. Whittlesey, July 1994. *Author*

Left:
A modern lightweight BR stop block of simple bolted construction. Cut sections of bullhead rail support a crossbeam of three horizontal rails with timber bolted to the front. In this bay-platform location, twin electric lights are provided. *Ray Ruffell*

Below:
Hydraulic buffers at the platform ends of Manchester Victoria in 1978. The various constructional details have been picked out in different colours and show up quite well. *R. Wildsmith*

Above:
The branch terminus at Middleton in Teesdale, Co Durham, boasted this North Eastern Railway stop block, again built of bullhead rail (note how it is cut to fit round the running rails). Flower boxes and an oil lamp adorn the neatly-shaped timber crossbeam. Two timber pads with hardwood facings are fitted to withstand buffer contact. *Ian Allan Library/John Topham*

Right:
Despite its antique appearance this is a 1994 view at Lowestoft, where an old installation has apparently been upgraded — but only slightly. The rounded-end timber beams are mounted directly on the platform face and carry centrally-placed red oil lamps. The beams and lamp cases are painted red. The buffers are standard-pattern wagon buffers bolted to the timbers. *Author*

CABLES

IN this context I refer to electrical cables of the type used mainly for colour light signalling installations and for certain traction applications, such as in the former Southern Railway territory equipped with third rail electrification.

Above:
Traction and certain heavy signalling cables, carried in concrete trunking at the lineside, are often carried up over the girders of bridges, as seen here. Note that the cables lie in channel section metal, mounted on brackets fitted to the timber parapet of the bridge. *BR/G. Marshall Smith*

CANOPIES (Station)

THE Victorian station architects believed in providing platform canopies to give passengers shelter between the train and the booking hall. Many of these canopies were splendid affairs supported on sturdy iron columns with varying amounts of decorative ironwork underpinning the roof. The canopy would sometimes be roofed with timber and coated with tar, but often would incorporate large glazed areas. The weight of the glass necessitated the very substantial supports.

Above:
The tiny wooden station building at Elsenham, junction for the Great Eastern Railway branch to Thaxted, sports a broad timber-covered canopy in this January 1979 view. Three cast-iron columns with decorative brackets carry the main girders of the canopy. The timber valancing is a distinctive GER feature. This station would, doubtless, have been extensively rebuilt with the Cambridge line electrification in the 1980s. *Andrew Muckley*

Right:
A single row of six very plain columns support this curved-roof canopy at Emerson Park Halt on the former London, Tilbury & Southend Railway line to Upminster. Cast spandrels carry steel beams on which the corrugated iron roof is mounted. Timber valancing makes for a neat structure which is quite straightforward to model using Plastruct section for the metal parts. A 24 January 1971 view. *J. M. Rickard*

Left:
The former London & South Western Railway station building at Virginia Water was demolished around 1970. This view shows a typical SR suburban station canopy, a lattice steel girder carried on three cast-iron columns supporting the peak-roofed structure. It is unglazed but roofed with asbestos sheets, an extremely heavy and brittle material. Red and white signs warning maintenance staff to use crawling or 'duck' boards when working on the roof would be displayed — probably on the face of the valancing. Note that the valancing along the front edge has had its 'points' removed, presumably either due to a clearance problem or in a bid to modernise its appearance. *Author*

Above:
Structural steelwork replaced iron for canopy construction in the latter part of the 19th century. This is a typical example of GWR 'standard' design: riveted steel columns carrying lattice steel girders and trusses. The roof covering is corrugated iron with timber, and later, steel, glazing bars. This example was at Bridgend. *Keith Willows*

Above:
A postwar British Railways canopy of typical design, reminiscent of an inverted umbrella. A simple frame of 'I' section steelwork supports an all-glazed roof, with drainage along the centre in the form of a valley gutter. This example at Shrewsbury was seen in about 1967. *Author*

Below:
This very neat steel-framed canopy on cast-iron columns was provided at Barnstaple Town station, built by the London & South Western Railway in 1898. Lynton & Barnstaple narrow gauge trains used the bay platform on the left. The distinctively-shaped gable end was altered by the Southern Railway with the addition of its standard timber valancing. *LGRP/Real Photographs*

CANOPY BRACKETS

THE cast-iron canopy bracket or spandrel was a feature of Victorian station design in which decorative structural ironwork was widely used. Platform canopies of substantial proportions and modest station porches would employ glazed roof structures supported on cast-iron columns carrying iron, steel or even timber beams. A very substantial structure was necessary to carry the weight of glazing in such a roof, and iron brackets springing from walls and columns were employed to stiffen the structure. Like the columns, the brackets would be a decorative feature with elaborate fretted patterns which would incorporate flowers, leaves, geometric patterns, railway initials or even coats of arms.

Such was the diversity of styles and sizes that only a few examples can be shown, but many examples still exist and those at operational stations nowadays tend to receive care and attention, including special painting to emphasise their details.

Below:
The initials of the London, Tilbury & Southend Railway are cast in the spandrels of these particularly elaborate canopy supports at Westcliff-on-Sea, seen in this photograph taken in November 1958 at the request of the Curator of Historical Relics. *BR*

Above:
At the opposite end of the scale, a timber canopy carried on beams extended from the roof trusses is seen here. There are no supporting columns, but cast-iron brackets bolted to the masonry help to support this simple awning at County School station. The intertwined initials of the Great Eastern Railway are incorporated in the design. County School station was restored from a derelict state and is now preserved. *Author*

CANOPY SUPPORT COLUMNS

LIKE the brackets, the supporting columns were treated by the Victorian architects as a feature to be used decoratively. Popular decorative devices include flowers, leaves and fir cones clustered at the top of the column — known in architectural terms as a 'decorated capital'. Early examples on the Great Western Railway — possibly a result of Brunel's classical influence — used a device called 'fasces', (a bundle of bound reeds which was a symbol of authority in Roman times) at the foot of the column. This appeared as a convex fluting overlaid with a spiral binding, and the wooden patterns for casting such a column can be found in the GWR Museum at Swindon.

Right:
A view at Staines West station during demolition work in 1981 provided an opportunity for a clear photograph of the complete column arrangement. The cast-iron column is slotted at the top to carry a substantial timber beam on which the roof structure was supported. The cast spandrels carry a circle with four oak leaves. Columns of this type and valancing of similar style were to be found on Great Eastern stations, but how they turned up on the Staines & West Drayton Railway, later part of the GWR, remains a mystery. Several of the columns from Staines West are now preserved at Didcot Railway Centre, whilst two remain on site, converted to lamp posts. *Author*

Above:
The valancing at Glemsford, GER, is similar to that at Staines West, but the columns are quite different, being of extremely heavy and rather short design, with lacy spandrels. The station closed in March 1967. *P. Hocquard*

CANOPY VALANCING

Left:
A view which shows well how the valancing brought the canopy as close as possible to the train in order to provide maximum protection from the weather. The Pressed Steel diesel railcar (Class 121) is awaiting departure from Staines West for West Drayton in 1964. *Author*

FOR the iron-framed, glazed canopy the 'icing on the cake' was the application of timber valancing around the edges, under the eaves of the structure. This disguised the ends of the supporting beams and provided rudimentary weather screening. In some instances guttering was incorporated, in others the valancing dispensed with the need for gutters. The valancing brought the canopy as close as possible to the train in order to provide weatherproof cover between the booking office and the train. Modern adaptations, where track and platforms have been altered, often mean that canopies have been removed or cut back or that platform edges have been moved out away from the canopy so that it no longer fulfils its original function properly.

The styles of valancing were incredibly varied, most railway companies having inherited a range of styles from their predecessors or from private companies and contractors. Some standard styles are certainly evident and for modellers in 4mm scale etched brass valancing strips are available from manufacturers such as Scalelink, Roxey Mouldings and Chris Leigh.

Left:
Despite the wide variety of valancing styles, similar examples did occur on different railways. In a 1960 scene, Maldon, GER, boasts valancing almost identical to Staines West, though somewhat deeper. WMD railbus No E79960 is waiting to depart for Witham. *L. Sandler*

CARRIAGE WASHERS

NOT an easy item to model, though some quite convincing models have been built using nylon brush bristles to represent the spray. The main features are a structure over the tracks in which the sprays and rotating brushes are mounted. Tanks would be provided nearby for water and chemicals. An operator's office would also be provided. The rails would be laid on a concrete apron with built-in drainage to carry away excess water.

Above:
A 1932 view of the LMS carriage-washing plant at Cricklewood. Coaching stock would be hauled through the plant for washing while *en route* to or from St Pancras station as empty stock. Carriage cleaning staff would check that all windows were closed before proceeding. *LMSR*

Left:
A two-track installation of similar vintage at Clapham Junction, SR, in 1935. Note the shape of the concrete apron. The operator is about to signal a train through the plant. *SR*

Right:
The Clapham Junction carriage washer after modernisation in 1949 showing the sprays in operation. Speed through the washer was restricted to just 3mph in order to give the chemicals and brushes time to work. *BR*

Centre right:
A smaller installation washes Bulleid main line stock at Ramsgate in 1956. The lack of any form of 'shed' over the installation was normal for these more modern structures. *BR*

Below:
Darlington in 1965 and here a separate 'portal' installation sprays the coaches with water before they enter the 'brush' unit in which rotating flails impregnated with 'Exmover' detergent clean the carriage sides. The post to the extreme right is a 'magic eye' device which sets the equipment in motion automatically as the train approaches. *BR*

Above:
The brush-unit and chemical storage tank section of the carriage washer at Bradford Hammerton Street depot washing a Metro-Cammell DMU. Rubber curtaining at the end of the unit reduces the spread of water so that only a minimal concrete apron is required to collect surplus water. *Dawson Bros*

Below:
A modern two-stage washer at Toton locomotive depot. The combination of grease and brake dust is notoriously difficult to remove from paintwork. The first section of this installation applies water and the 'Exmover' detergent which is then given time to work before the locomotive passes through the second, brushing and rinsing, stage. The life of paintwork is prolonged if the powerful cleaning agents are fully removed after washing. *BR*

Above:
The photoelectric equipment mounted on the three left-hand posts controls the automatic operation of this carriage cleaner for electric units at Southend-on-Sea. The chequer-pattern signs denote limited clearance, warning staff not to lean out of the train. A 1960 view. *BR*

Below:
The three sets of rotating flails are clearly seen in this view at Leeds Neville Hill in May 1969. Note the ladders and walkways, and the customary concrete apron and rubber curtains. Water is sprayed at 350 gallons per minute. *BR*

CATCH POINTS

CATCH points are provided in sidings where rolling stock might run away on to a main line. They are simply a means of derailing a runaway vehicle before it can do any harm. Today, some sidings are protected by the use of a 'derail' which is simply a hinged metal block which can be locked into place on the rail to perform the same function without the complexity of using a turn-out.

Right and below:
Two views of the catch point at Black Dog Siding on the Calne branch in the 1950s, showing the points set to derail any runaway wagons before they could obstruct the running line on the left. *Don Lovelock*

CATENARY

CATENARY — overhead line equipment — is a difficult subject for the modeller and a complex feature of the modern railway. It is also distinctive to the system employed and fortunately the UK has seen only two significantly different main-line installations in large-scale use. These are the now obsolete 1,500V dc electrification originated by the LNER and used primarily on the Manchester–Sheffield (Woodhead) route, and the 25kV ac electrification settled on as standard by BR in the 1950s and used on East and West Coast main lines plus the GN suburban, Midland suburban and East Anglian electrification schemes. A fundamental difference between the two systems is that the more modern high-voltage system requires a lighter-weight installation than did the 1,500V dc system. Indeed, it was renewal costs of masts and fixed equipment, set against declining traffic, which sealed the fate of the Woodhead route and saw its closure in the 1970s.

Below:
Lattice spans are used in a station area such as at Stafford where a very wide span with few posts is required. This view from the front of a train shows the drop-arms and insulators extremely well. This is 25kV ac electrification on the West Coast main line. *BR*

Above:
The Kent Coast electrification provided a number of goods yards where the 750V dc current for the Class 71 electric locomotives was taken from overhead wires rather than from the third rail, in order to protect shunters and other railwaymen who worked on the ground. With continental ferry wagons in tow, electric locomotive No E5001 is seen operating off the overhead catenary in Hither Green yard. The advent of electro-diesel locomotives (which use either electric or diesel), rendered the overhead system redundant. *BR*

Centre left:
Lattice portal spans with lightweight tubular drop-arms are employed here at Nuneaton Trent Valley, seen in 1964. *BR*

Below left:
An end post with pulleys and tensioning weights on the 25kV ac East Coast main line electrification at Peterborough. *Author*

CATTLE DOCKS

ONCE a feature of numerous rural stations, the cattle dock was a separate platform with pens where livestock could be contained temporarily while loading or unloading from rail wagons. Cattle markets were often located close by the station so that animals could be transferred easily between train and market.

Usually, the cattle dock was brick-paved with a surface designed to reduce the risk of animals slipping and with built-in drainage gullies. There would be a tap for watering and the pens were normally made of round steel horizontal bars on concrete or steel posts. A lime wash was used for cleaning down after use, giving brickwork a whitened appearance. An excellent plastic kit for a later-style GWR cattle dock is available in 4mm scale from Ratio.

Right:
The GWR used redundant bridge rail for a variety of purposes. A common use was for the construction of the pens on a cattle dock as seen here at Moretonhampstead in 1959. Note the boarded and paved section of track beside the dock — this was where the debris was washed off the dock.
M. Windeatt

Below:
A disused cattle dock with posts and railings of timber, at Buntingford, GER, in the late 1950s. *A. Lawrence*

COALING STAGES

AT locomotive depots and sheds where locomotives were serviced or stabled overnight, it was necessary to provide facilities for watering and coaling. Mechanised coaling devices could not be justified and the locomotive coal was often shovelled direct from a wagon into the bunker of the locomotive. However, where this was not done, a coaling stage would be provided to enable the locomotive crew to reach more easily when shovelling the coal by hand from a stockpile into the locomotive. The coaling stage would usually be a short platform of timber, brick or stone construction, with the coal simply piled on one end.

Above:
The coaling stage at its simplest. Brick piers support a timber platform on which the coal is piled ready for loading. The location is Wisbech, in the early 1950s. No 68225 was among the last 'J70' 0-6-0Ts retained there for working the tramway to Upwell. All were moved away in August 1952. *LGRP*

Left:
Built entirely of timber, the coaling stage at Redditch had a small covered area for storage, and an oil lamp.
R. J. Essery

Above:
GER 'J15' 0-6-0 No 65467 stands at Aldeburgh coaling stage on 13 July 1955. The stage here is built of brick and surfaced with concrete. In the background are the engine shed and water tank. *E. Brookes*

Below:
The GWR used soft Welsh coal which could not be dropped from coaling towers, so a satisfactory method of hand-coaling for large depots had to be developed. The standard coaling stage incorporated a massive water tank on top of the brick-built structure. Wagons of coal were run up a siding into the structure and their contents off-loaded into small four-wheeled tubs. The platforms seen here above the locomotive cab, were folded out over the tender. The tubs were then run out on to them and tipped to fill the tender. *T. G. Cousens*

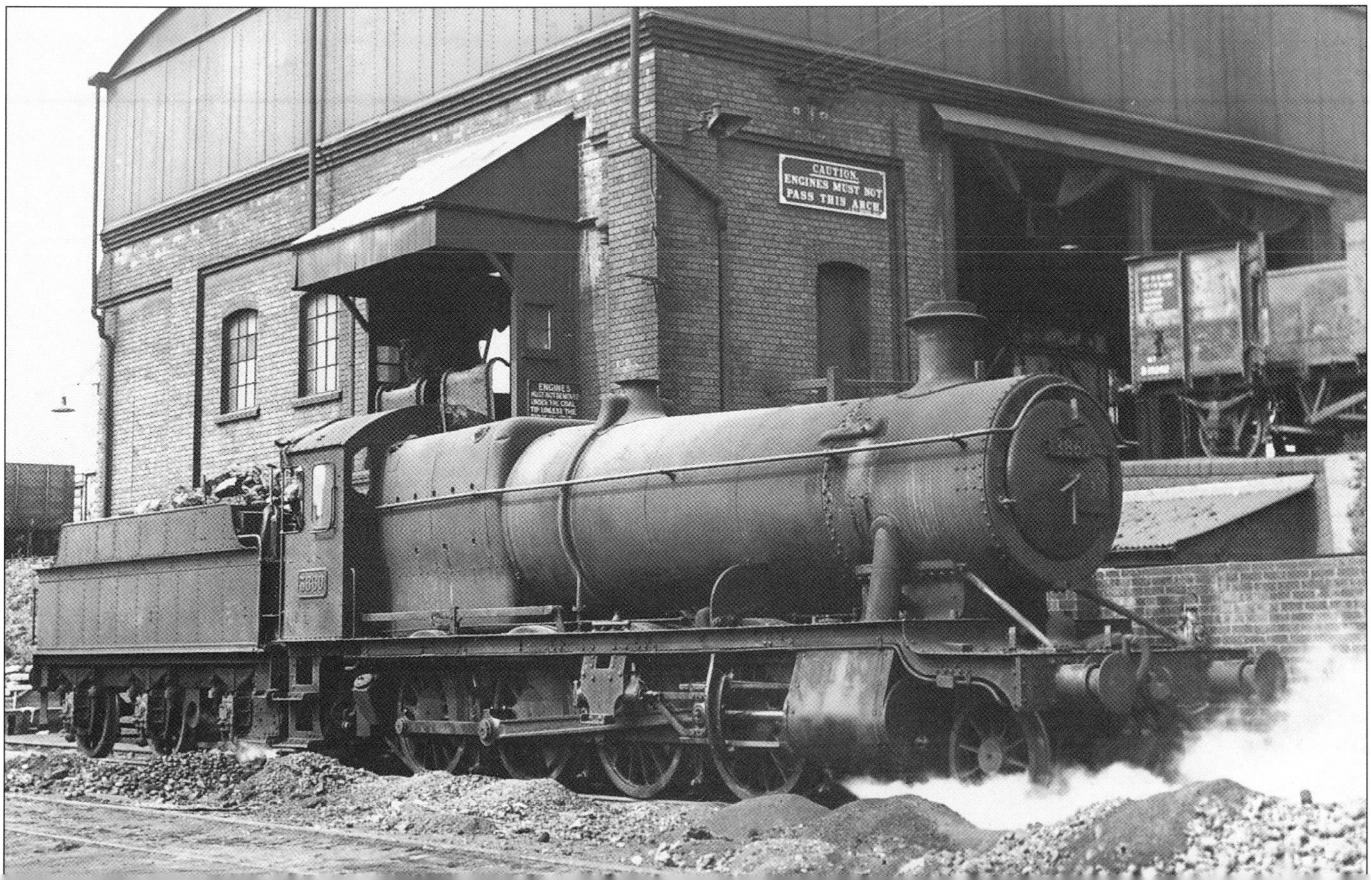

COALING TOWERS

THE provision of mechanised coaling was necessary at all large depots where substantial numbers of locomotives were being fuelled and watered every day. Early coaling plants were still fairly manual, consisting of gantries under which a locomotive would be parked to enable wheeled 'tubs' of coal to be pushed out over the tender and tipped by hand. This system persisted on the Great Western Railway and the Western Region through to the end of steam because the soft Welsh steam coal which GWR locomotives burned would be broken into dust by dropping from a high mechanical coaling plant.

The latter were, however, familiar on all the other regions, the LMS going in for some particularly tall concrete structures. In these, the wagons of coal were hoisted individually to the top of the tower and their contents tipped into a vast hopper. This then dispensed coal by the tenderful to locomotives stopped beneath it.

The last surviving LMS coal tower is at Carnforth, Lancashire, but it is believed that the structure is no longer safe to use.

Above left:
The familiar LMS coaling tower is typified by this example at Toton: in effect, a large elevated hopper. A wagon is being lifted up the outside of the tower for tipping. Engines would be loaded with a predetermined amount. *LMS*

Left:
An LMS coaling tower of modest proportions, photographed in 1932. The wagon (right) is lifted and upturned to empty its contents into a hopper. From this, the coal is fed up a covered conveyor belt into the tower from where it is a short drop into the tender. *Ian Allan Library*

Above:
The LNER coaling tower at Kipps is a similar concrete hopper to the Toton example, but lacks the wagon-lifting apparatus of the LMS type. Here, the wagon can be seen being emptied into a bin behind the plant from where it would be raised into the hopper by conveyor. *Ian Allan Library*

Above right:
A 'WD' 2-8-0 stands under the coaler at Thornton Junction MPD in August 1966. Coaling towers are seldom modelled because few layouts have space for a large motive-power depot, but convincingly constructed, they make for impressive models. *G. P. Cooper*

Right:
The coaling tower at Patricroft shed was the LMS pattern with an external wagon lift. It is seen here near the end of its working life in June 1967. *M. S. Stokes*

CRANES

THE goods yard crane was a universal requirement in yards large and small. It varied from the massive travelling cranes seen usually on the docks for transferring goods from rail to ship, down to hand cranes of scarcely 1-ton capacity in rural goods yards.

Right:
A superbly elegant little hand crane in the yard at Whitney-on-Wye in May 1963. *Author's collection*

Below:
Another fine example of a small hand crane. This timber derrick was still in Wellingborough goods shed in 1979.
R. Payne

CRANES (Portal)

THE portal crane comprises a gantry which spans several railway sidings and usually runs on a pair of widely-spaced rails. A traversing lifting hook or cradle is suspended from the gantry. The portal crane is most commonly used in modern container terminals for transferring containers from rail to road or vice versa.

Above:
A very early form of 'travelling crane' as used by the LMS in an unidentified goods yard. The operator's cabin is built of corrugated iron and traverses with the lifting hook and cradle which are slung beneath it. Since the operator cannot see directly below him, precise positioning cannot have been easy. *Ian Allan Library*

Above:
This Stothert & Pitt portal crane photographed at Parkeston Quay Freightliner terminal in August 1968 represents the more modern type of travelling crane, specifically designed to deal with standard containers. The operator's cabin is suspended on an arm alongside the lifting tackle so that he can see precisely what he is doing. The lifting cradle is a sophisticated set of hydraulic arms which engage the lifting eyes on the corners of the container. The safe working load (SWL) is shown as 30 tons. *BR*

Below:
A pair of cranes at the Folingsby terminal, Tyne & Wear, which closed in 1987, seen just before the closure. Less elegant than the Parkeston Quay example, these utilitarian cranes show clearly the lifting cradle and, on the farther crane, the operator's cabin positioned perfectly for controlling the lifting process. A plastic kit for a container crane has been available, it is believed, in the Peco/Merit range. *I. S. Carr*

CROSSINGS (Accommodation)

THE accommodation crossing was normally provided to enable farm machinery or livestock to be moved across the line where a railway had bisected farm fields, without the provision of expensive signalling. Bridges under or over the line were always preferred, but in fairly flat locations bridging was sometimes impractical. Here, the accommodation crossing — a minimum cost level crossing with no signalling or other protection — was provided. It was usually the responsibility of the farmer to satisfy himself that it was safe to cross. Usually the crossings were maintained by agreement with the landowner without there necessarily being any public right of way.

Typically they consist of a board crossing on the railway, reached by a typical farm gate of the five-barred type. On the modern railway the only real change, apart from modern warning signs, would be the provision of galvanised metal farm gates.

Where such crossings serve public footpaths a traditional stile would be provided on either side of the line instead of, or in addition to, the farm gates.

Below:
The three views included here all illustrate the same accommodation crossing at Kirland near Bodmin and were taken by the Western Region in 1957. This view, looking north, shows the crossing apparently before repairs which involved levelling the approaches. The gate leads directly into a flat field and carries a GWR-era warning notice regarding the penalty for failing to close it. *BR*

Above:
The second view shows the crossing after improvement and looking the opposite way, illustrating that the field on that side of the line drops away steeply. *BR*

Below:
The third view, looking along the railway, shows the newly-installed timbers. The lack of any cattle grids beside the crossing suggests that it was only intended for use by farm machinery. *BR*

CROSSINGS (Barrier)

THE lifting-barrier crossing came about because of the need for a system which could be remotely controlled. The installation of multiple-aspect colour light signalling controlled from a handful of signalling centres meant that many level crossings would be miles from the signalbox which controlled them. The lifting barrier is easier than swing-gates to operate electrically and is also safer, in that it opens upwards, away from potential obstructions.

Though lifting barriers had been used throughout the world, the gated crossing remained the norm in the UK until the advent of widespread signalling modernisation in the 1960s. Full-barrier crossings are used on heavily trafficked roads with control either from an adjacent signalbox, or by closed circuit TV from a remote signalbox.

Above:
An early installation of lifting barriers, indeed, the very first of their kind in Britain, were those at Warthill, Yorkshire, seen here when new in November 1952. The provision of such crossings required changes in the highway laws and these required that flashing warning lights, stop signs and floodlighting be provided. A folding barrier (skirt) is suspended from the main pole to prevent small children and animals from straying under the barrier. *BR*

Above:
By June 1962 the lifting-barrier crossing had become more like the version which is familiar today. This installation seen at Stallingborough in June 1962 is a half-barrier crossing (ie with barriers protecting only the approach sides of the crossing) and is automatically operated by an approaching train. The barrier is striped with red and white reflective strips and the flashing warning lights have a rectangular black backplate. Half-barriers do not have skirts and are restricted to less heavily used crossings which can be satisfactorily controlled by an electronic switching mechanism on the track. *BR*

Below:
Here is a modern full-width barrier crossing on the Yate–Tytherington branch, seen in 1972. The presence of skirts under the barrier means that this crossing is manually controlled, either from a signalbox or, in this case, most probably by a member of the train crew alighting and operating the barrier from a local control cabinet. Note that in the aftermath of the serious accident at Hixon crossing, the warning lights have an additional flashing amber light to give advance warning, and that the backplate has a yellow border. There would also be an audible warning sounding from the moment that the lights operate until the barriers rise again. *BR*

Above:
The crossing at Oulton Broad North station is a full-barrier type operated from the adjacent signalbox. In a typical station installation the barriers are protected by a wooden picket fence. The statutory single amber and double flashing red warning lights are arranged in the 'normal' layout — some installations require the lights to be mounted in a vertical line. *Author*

Above right:
Another 1994 view of the crossing at Oulton Broad North, showing the picket fence arrangement and the separate pedestrian gate. Small red lights are mounted on the barrier as an additional night-time warning to road users. *Author*

Above:
The road surface of the Oulton Broad North crossing shows the standard surfacing material, the entire road area of the crossing being cross-hatched with yellow lining to warn road users not to stop on the crossing. At either side of the roadway are pedestrian walkways and outside these a timber 'cattle grid' is provided as a deterrent to trespassers. *Author*

CROSSINGS (Gated)

ANYONE who remembers the steam era will almost certainly remember with affection (or irritation if he was a motorist) the gated level crossing, with its huge white wooden gates controlled from an adjacent signalbox. In such locations the signalman not only had the movement and signalling of trains under his control but he also had to keep road traffic moving. The gates were controlled from the 'box by a large capstan wheel which operated a complex system of steel rods and bevel gears to transform its rotary motion into the quadrant swing of up to four gates.

The wheels and mechanisms differed substantially from one railway to another and between the various different private manufacturers of signalling equipment. The heavy cast wheel imparted a 'fly-wheel'-like momentum which eased the burden on the signalman who might have to operate his gates a dozen or more times every hour.

In its simplest form the gates of such a crossing were operated by hand, a gate-keeper being employed to open and close them. Such gates were often only pairs, but each gate would be very long. They would be hung to the posts in such a way as to minimise the distance which the operator had to walk. As he closed one, the opening latch of the other would be close at hand.

Below:
The standard Great Western level crossing, seen here at Colnbrook in 1964. The gates provided for double-track (never laid) and the line crossed the busy Bath Road (A4) until a by-pass was built. The horizontal spars of the gates are tapered, the hinges and gate posts being very substantial castings. Separate wicket gates, lockable from the signalbox, were provided for pedestrians. *Author's collection*

Above:
The standard Southern Railway gate, as seen at Baynards in the mid-1960s, was a less elaborate affair with parallel timbers and was suspended from square concrete posts. A distinctive feature was the large red and white warning disc, fitted half to each gate. Metal stay-rods from the hinge to the lower corner of the gate helped to support the very substantial weight. *Ian Allan Library*

Below:
A rear view of the standard SR crossing gates at Betchworth station, taken in the mid-1960s. Parallel timbers are used throughout, with distinctive 'X'-shaped bracing and black-painted wire ironwork, including the wire stays. Depending upon the levels of rail and road traffic, such gates could be hand-operated or worked by a capstan wheel in an adjacent signalbox. Another distinctive SR feature in this view is the upper quadrant semaphore starting signal with its posts built from two sections of bullhead rail. *Ian Allan Library*

Above:
Taken in December 1954 to illustrate a very modern footbridge installation, this view shows the level crossing gates at Bathgate on the Scottish Region. This is a former North British Railway crossing, with timber gates having a single diagonal cross-brace and unusual diamond-shaped red warning signs. The gate is hinged from substantial iron castings and has a long wire stay-rod. Separate pedestrian wicket gates are provided. *BR*

Left:
The former LNWR gated crossing at Wansford is one of the few wheel-operated crossings to survive in preservation. This view shows the timber gates with slightly tapered main beams and pairs of timber 'X' bracing. Metal rods prevent small children or animals from climbing through the gates. The gate locks which rise from the road and engage iron catches on the gates can be seen at the foot of the picture. *Author*

Below:
A full view of Wansford crossing which is controlled by a capstan wheel in the signalbox (right). Note that the gates differ slightly, one having three 'X' braces and the other only two. Gates were purpose-built for their locations and some crossings required gates of widely differing dimensions. *Author*

Right:
The modern gated crossing at Stewartby employs hand-operated metal gates hung on metal posts. The crossing keeper has control of signals protecting the crossing and is advised of approaching trains by bell signals from the next proper signalbox in either direction. Note that the gates are hung on metal posts (right) and iron-capped wooden posts (left). The pedestrian walkway is ungated. *Author*

Centre right:
Another view of Stewartby which is mainly of interest to show the construction of the road surface. It is entirely made of timbers laid parallel with the rails. Sometimes timbers are used only within the 'four-foot' way, either tarmac or modern rubberised surfacing being used for the rest of the surface. Many modern crossings are also cross-hatched with yellow 'no-stopping' lines as an additional warning to road users. *Author*

Below:
A typical Great Eastern Railway hand-operated gate across two tracks, in this case the disused Fakenham & Dereham line at North Elmham. The very long single gate has parallel timbers with five 'X' braces and still relies for its structural integrity upon a long hinged stay-wire attached to, and bolted right through, an enormous timber post. Note the timber warning disc which is starting to fall to pieces. A 1994 view. *Author*

Left:
A similar pattern of GER hand-operated gated crossing still exists at Whittlesey, near Peterborough. The gates here are even longer, with six 'X' braces and the stay-wires suspended from hefty concrete posts. A track-circuited tubular post starter signal protects the crossing and is controlled from a signalbox some 200yd away behind the photographer. Here, the crossing keeper has responsibility only for opening and closing the gates. Note that the blend of old and new here would make for interesting modelling, particularly as the platforms are barely two-coach lengths. *Author*

Centre left:
A detailed view of one of the Whittlesey gates. Note the signal beyond with its square black sighting board to eliminate confusing background structures. *Author*

Bottom left:
The road user's view of Whittlesey crossing with its picket fencing and pedestrian wicket gates. The scale of the concrete gate post is apparent in this view. *Author*

Right:
A GER hand-operated crossing seen in its station setting at Fakenham East on 28 August 1974. The gate is similar to that at North Elmham, but with a concrete post. *R. A. King*

Centre right:
This August 1968 view of the crossing at Morar, first station outside Mallaig on the West Highland extension, is a far cry from what's there today. Two splendid lower quadrant, lattice-post semaphore signals protect a little road crossing with white five-barred gates. The crossing keeper's signal cabin was apparently out of use by this time and the signals appear to be operated by the weighted ground levers visible in front of the left-hand gate post. *C. Lofthus*

Bottom right:
The GWR standard crossing in what must be one of its smallest installations — all the more remarkable in that it still survives. St Mary's Crossing, Stroud, once boasted its own halt but now only the crossing and signalbox survive. The tiny crossing is closed to road traffic except when road users ring the bell for attention. Then, the crossing keeper will open the gates by hand if it is safe to do so. No protecting signals are provided and the separate wicket gates are not lockable. *Author*

Above:
An unusual crossing layout existed at Wisbech North on the Midland & Great Northern Joint line, where the road crossed the railway at an oblique angle. The gates are not unlike those of the GER, but with square 'X'-brace sections, a tall, more elaborate concrete post and twin stay-wires. Note the wicket gate beside the signalbox. In this type of installation the gates were sometimes too short to close off the railway completely when they were open for road traffic.
Frank Church

Below:
Most of the old LNWR gates on the Bedford–Bletchley line have since been replaced with BR-built metal gates (see Stewartby, earlier in this section) but this August 1974 view shows how they used to look. This dilapidated example was at Bow Brickhill halt. Note the large wooden 'gate-stop' between the running lines. *Kevin Lane*

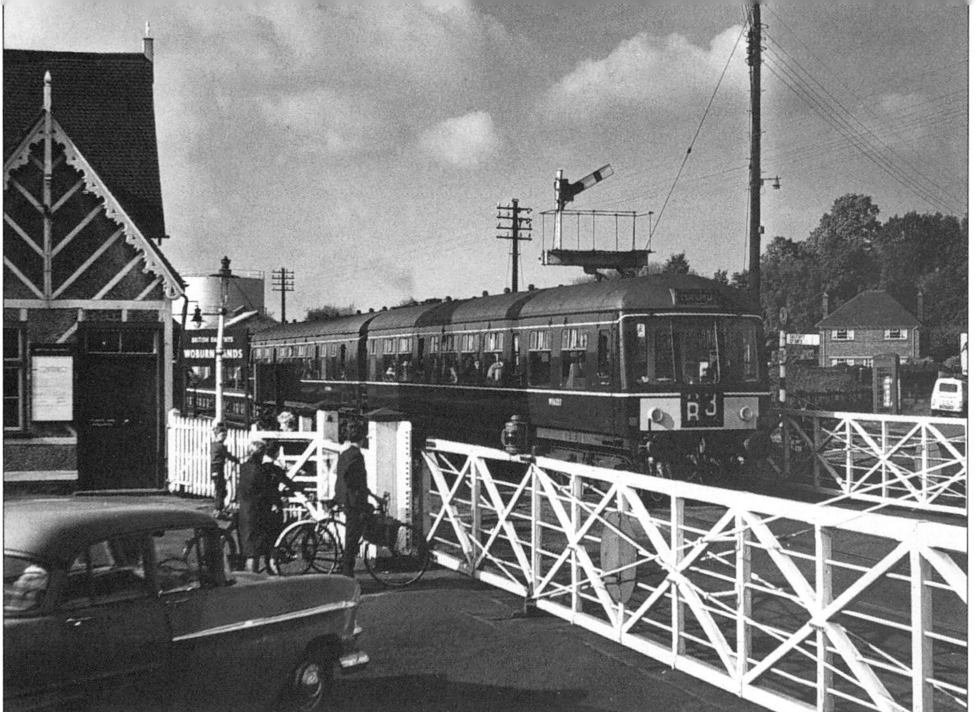

Right:
Much larger, capstan-wheel-operated, swing gates existed on the same line at Woburn Sands station, as seen here, where a long and a short gate are required to close off a wide roadway. These have since been replaced by lifting barriers.
E. J. S. Gadsden

Centre right:
At the tiny crossing outside Pitsea station on the Tilbury line, the nearer gate opened away from the railway and the far gate was set well away from the line, so the railway was not closed off at all when the gates were open to road traffic. In readiness for the installation of overhead catenary, a string of cowbells has been erected over the road to provide a warning to high vehicles. *Frank Church*

Below:
LBSCR gates with six horizontal bars were operated from the signalbox at Goring-by-Sea as seen in this August 1969 view. The standard SR red metal roundels are fitted. *J. Scrace*

CROSSINGS (Open)

UNGATED crossings have always been restricted to crossings of minor roads by little-used railway lines, though in recent years the 'open crossing' with warning signs has become more widespread. At these the train is usually required to stop or proceed at very low speed while crossing the road, and warning lights operate to alert road traffic.

In steam days the ungated crossing would be provided with little more than the statutory road sign 'Trains cross here' and was restricted mainly to goods branches and industrial railways used by infrequent and slow trains.

Above:
A 1983 view of Naas crossing, between Newport and Gloucester, shows the warning lights in operation, and clearly illustrates the road markings. Of particular interest are the various warning notices. These are standard at all modern crossings and those concerning large and slow vehicles were the result of the Hixon accident in which a large transformer-carrying lorry was struck by a train after grounding on an uneven crossing. *BR*

Right:
These two views of Seaton Bank Head crossing illustrate perfectly the open crossing of both the steam and 'modern' era for they show the same location from the same viewpoint before and after modernisation. Originally the crossing was ungated and protected only by rudimentary warning signs. The modern lamp post seen in the 'before' view is part of the new installation. *I. S. Carr*

Below left:
By 27 May 1984 the track has been singled, the footbridge removed (as were footbridges at many crossings where lifting barriers were installed) and the crossing is protected by 'cross-buck' signs and flashing lights on both sides of the road. *I. S. Carr*

Top:
Two views which show the open crossing at Quintrell Downs on the Newquay branch in the mid-1980s. This picture shows the whole installation with lights and picket fencing, and the original crossing keeper's cottage in the background. *Author*

Above:
This second view shows the light units and the road markings as a Class 142 DMU crosses the road. *Author*

Left:
A crossing of the North Devon & Cornwall Junction line (Torrington–Halwill Junction) at Watergate halt was an ungated open crossing which dated from the construction of the line in the 1920s and is here seen in 1964. This view shows well the triangular timbers used to form a cattle grid to prevent animals from straying on to the line.
O. H. Prosser

Below:
Perhaps the ultimate in ramshackle open crossings was this example at Wick St Lawrence on the Weston, Clevedon & Portishead Railway — an impecunious outfit which was closed in 1940. The crumbling road surface is bounded on either side by a crude cattle grid. *Real Photographs*

CULVERTS

THIS category takes in all those under-line passages from large drainage pipes up to small bridges. Culverts are essentially a part of land-drainage systems although they sometimes serve the dual purpose of providing a 'cattle-creep' to enable livestock to pass safely under the line. See **Bridges (Under Rails).**

CUTTINGS

THE requirement to minimise gradients led the railway engineers to dig through, or go round, hills and sometimes to tunnel under them. Usually the approach to a tunnel would be by way of a gradually deepening cutting and on any model it is important to make the 'lie of the land' convincing. Dependent upon the substrata, cuttings could be dug through soft material, as Brunel's navvies did at Sonning, or hewn through rock blasted away with explosives. Either way, such heavy engineering was time-consuming and expensive.

Where soft ground was excavated for cuttings, the sides of the cutting would have a shallow slope — perhaps 30° or less — with grass, bushes and trees growing on them. In the steam era the growth would be cut back from the track to reduce the fire risk. In rock cuttings the sides would be self-supporting and thus they could be almost vertical. There might be combinations, too, where the top-soil layer is quite thin and the cutting goes through into rock. Here the cutting would have steep rock walls topped by a shallow-sloping grass bank.

In soft terrain where there was a restriction on width, which prevented shallow sloping sides, the engineers would build retaining walls of brick or stone to hold back the ground and prevent landslips onto the track. Brick retaining walls are built of very hard engineers' bricks — impervious to water and frost damage — and are usually buttressed and arched in order to strengthen them. They are, too, not usually vertical but leaning slightly against the material which they are holding back.

See also section headed **Embankments.**

Below:
Examples of cuttings cut through stone can be seen in numerous places such as, illustrated here, the West Highland extension from Fort William to Mallaig. BR Standard Class 4 2-6-0 No 76001 heads towards Fort William at Arisaig with an evening departure from Mallaig in June 1960. *Ian Allan Library*

Above:
Class A3 4-6-2 No 60039 *Sandwich* passes through Hadley Wood, and its cutting, with the Fridays Only 6.5pm King's Cross-Leeds/Bradford service. *Gerald T. Robinson*

Below:
Arguably the most dramatic example of a cutting provided with retaining walls and supports is to be found near Roade in Northamptonshire. At this point the West Coast main line (visible on the right at a slightly higher level) heads towards Rugby whilst the Northampton line (on the left) heads off to the north. In August 1982 Class 85 No 85035 is pictured on a down express running towards Rugby and Coventry. *Michael Ricks*

DEPARTURE BOARDS

DISPLAYS to indicate the destination of forthcoming trains were normally provided at the larger stations or at those where trains divided for several different routes. In the steam era the wooden 'finger' board inserted into an upright post by platform staff was the simplest form of indicator. At main stations complicated electro-mechanical departure boards were provided and these changed constantly as trains came and went.

A development of the 1960s was the Solari indicator, again more usual at large stations, though some small installations were provided at suburban stations. These displays were controlled by signalling centres, often many miles away. The most modern form of departure indicator is the closed circuit TV monitor. Large stations now have batteries of these orange-painted monitors on every platform.

Below:
A night-time view at Manchester Victoria shows a fine example of the 'finger' board with alternative boards in the rack. The clock shows the 9.18pm departure time of the train to Bury, Accrington, Burnley and Nelson & Colne — the next service from the adjacent platform. *John Clarke*

Below:
The severed platform canopy at Reading reveals the modern style of departure indicator: a digital clock display with an orange-painted TV monitor alongside displaying the destination and departure time of the next train from that platform. *Author*

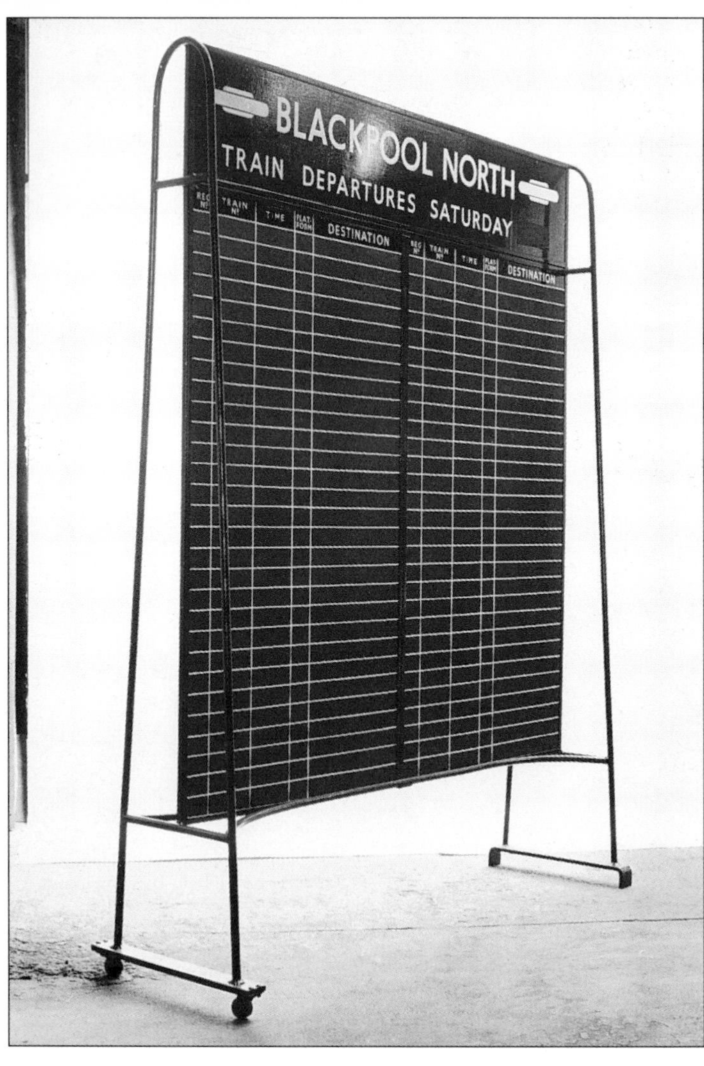

Above left:
A departure board of very simple form was an innovation at Blackpool North in June 1953, as seen here in an official view. The blackboard is mounted on a wheeled frame so that it can be moved into an appropriate position. *BR*

Above:
A next train indicator as provided at the platform barriers on Birmingham New Street in 1955. The display is simple and informative, with the departure time clearly shown and a full list of stopping places. *BR*

Left:
The platform supervisor changes train information on a modern electrically-operated departure board. Locally controlled boards of this type have been superseded by the electronic displays operated from signalling control centres. *Modern Transport*

EMBANKMENTS

EMBANKMENTS and cuttings are the two features of railway civil engineering which need to be considered together. In driving a railway route through undulating countryside, and minimising gradients so that conventional steam traction could be employed, the engineers cut through hills and built embankments across valleys. Just as long cuttings and gradients usually led to a tunnel, so embankments would be frequently pierced by bridges (for roads and water-courses) and sometimes by magnificent viaducts.

The careful railway engineer would endeavour to keep the amount of cuttings and embankments roughly equal. In that way, the spoil from cuttings could be used to build embankments. If there were lots of embankments but few cuttings, the engineer would have insufficient 'fill' material and would have to resort to 'side cutting' — an expensive process which usually involved excavating material from nearby pits or quarries. If the reverse were true, then thousands of tons of unwanted spoil would have to be transported away.

See also section headed **Cuttings.**

Above:
Typical of embankments throughout Britain is this stretch of line on the ex-Great Western Bristol-Frome route at Limpley Stoke. On 26 March 1962 'Hall' class 4-6-0 No 5924 *Dinton Hall* heads south with a passenger train. *I. G. Shearing*

ENGINE SHEDS

THE subject of locomotive sheds could fill a book in itself and indeed there are many such books available, dealing in detail with the sheds of one company or even with individual major depots. This section deals mainly with small engine sheds suitable for the average layout and these are generally one- or two-track sheds with accommodation for just a couple of engines.

Right:
The single-road engine shed at Much Wenlock, GWR, was brick-built with its water tank mounted on one end (a locomotive parked underneath and kept in steam would keep the tank from freezing in winter). The slatted roof ventilator was necessary to release engine smoke. Round-topped entrances were quite common, but the Much Wenlock shed is rather longer than normal, as it was used to house a steam railmotor when these operated the branch from Wellington. *Author's collection*

Below:
The rather basic little North Eastern Railway shed at Middleton in Teesdale was stone-built and had the obligatory roof ventilator, plus round-topped entrance and timber doors which fitted closely around the rails. *Real Photographs (K3210)*

Above:
The ventilator on the roof of Moretonhampstead shed extends the full length of the roof and the stone-built structure has a round-topped entrance apparently without doors by this time. The signalbox is brick-built in the form of a lean-to against the shed, while a single-storey rear extension provides a simple messroom for the crew. Note the coal bunker to the right of the shed entrance. *N. L. M. Stone*

Centre right:
A rear view of the neat little shed at Tetbury, GWR, shows the water tank, raised from its original height on newer brickwork, and the water crane with its brazier below. The branch engine, '58XX' 0-4-2T No 5804, is about to go on shed after its day's work.
N. E. Preedy

Bottom right:
A general view of Tetbury shed after closure shows square-topped doors and windows, a single smoke vent in the roof and on the left the remains of the wooden coaling stage. *Author*

Left:
An excellent view of the whole locomotive shed provision at Malmesbury, Wiltshire. The stone shed has horizontal planking to the left of the entrance which shows that it was originally built for the broad gauge (7ft). Outside, a metal water tank stands on columns over the timber coaling stage. Malmesbury shed survives as a motor car tyre centre — the only vestige of the railway left at this site. *Real Photographs (19732)*

Centre left:
A '14XX' class 0-4-2T is scarcely visible in the dingy depths of the crumbling timber shed at Staines West. A crude structure, with no adequate smoke ventilation, its windows are opaque with filth. A separate conical water tank is provided and the only mess facilities are inside a grounded 'Toad' brake-van body. *Real Photographs*

Below:
This view of the engine shed at Clevedon on the Weston, Clevedon & Portishead Railway in 1937 shows the whole installation, including a rather shabby shed, water tank and the coal stock — surprisingly large for an impecunious little light railway. *Real Photographs*

EQUIPMENT CABINETS

EVERYTHING from lockable cupboards up to small huts is really covered by this description, for the railway still uses a variety of means to keep lineside equipment weatherproof and secure against vandalism and interference. Equipment cabinets have, for example, long been required for such things as the batteries used to power signal instruments in locations where there was no mains electricity supply. The modern railway has made the equipment cabinet an art form, for not only is there a greater need for remote electrical equipment for unmanned items such as level crossing barriers and electrically-operated points, there has also been a growth in little-used equipment operated by train crews, such as crossing warning lights on freight-only lines. Sadly, the increasing vandalism and interference has meant that such installations now have to be very secure indeed.

Above:
A 1952 picture of a then new automatic signalling installation between Thornton Heath and Norbury on the Southern Region. A variety of shapes and sizes of steel cabinet are used here, while the small striped box contains a telephone. *BR*

Left:
More modern electrical equipment cabinets used probably for point operation or track-circuit equipment, on a semaphore-signalled line at Whittlesey, between March and Peterborough. A 1994 view. *Author*

Above:
Bearing the hallmarks of modern life, an equipment cabinet which was installed in 1981 at Staines West. Providing track circuits and a ground signal controlling egress from the siding it is operated remotely from Feltham Panel signalbox. *Author*

Above:
The modern (1980s) lineside telephone box. This example at Staines West enabled train crews to notify Feltham Panel when they were ready to leave the siding. *Author*

FENCING (Lineside)

LINESIDE fencing is an important feature of the British railway scene, for only in the UK are railways required by law to erect and maintain continuous fences on both sides of their running lines. Thus, in Britain, the unfenced railway is rare. Fencing was often distinctive to the owning railway, some using particular styles of wooden fencing or iron railings. One distinctive type was the Great Western Railway's use of six strands of wire attached to timber posts with corner posts of bridge rails and occasional 'tensioning' devices. The Great Eastern used distinctive heavy timbers with a 45° pointed top.

Above:
Even the lowliest of light railways were required to have their lines fully fenced. Unsawn 'rustic' posts with several strands of wire serve the Bishop's Castle Railway in this rural backwater. *Author's collection*

Right:
Square wooden posts with the tops tapered on two sides were standard on the GWR, as was the spacing of the six strands of wire, with the three lowest wires closer together to prevent smaller animals such as lambs from passing through. '4575' class 2-6-2T No 5540 is entering Black Dog halt from Chippenham in the mid-1950s.
Don Lovelock

Above:
A young lad watches the passage of a Class 20-hauled local goods on a former NER line protected by stout posts carrying four horizontal timbers, at the approach to a public road crossing. A splendid cast-iron trespass notice presides over the scene. *M. A. Smyth*

Below:
Posts and wire protect the lineside on this section of the former Great Eastern Railway as Class 40 No 40074 passes Haughley Junction with a Paisley–Parkeston Quay freight in November 1982. The approach to the road crossing has more substantial protection in the form of white-painted wooden palings. *John C. Baker*

FOOTBRIDGES

THE railways provided footbridges to link station platforms and, on busy roads, as a means for pedestrians to avoid lengthy waits at level crossings. In some instances railway footbridges were also provided to carry footpaths and other rights of way over the line.

Many railway companies had standard designs of footbridge and there were some very handsome structures which lasted from the Victorian era until well into BR days. Indeed, some early examples still exist, although the advent of automatic level crossings has dispensed with the need for many footbridges at such locations. The requirements of disabled access have also tended to militate against the old-style footbridge with its steep stairs, while cutbacks in maintenance budgets have spelt the end for other footbridges. Nevertheless, there are still many to be seen, although outside preserved railways, comparatively few survive in their original condition.

Right:
This handsome curved lattice footbridge at Evesham Midland station was a standard Midland Railway pattern. It has intermediate landings supported on groups of four cast-iron columns, the second flight of stairs being carried on the curved section of the span. An etched brass kit for a very similar footbridge was produced in 4mm scale by George Alan but is now out of production.
Author's collection

Left:
This Highland Railway footbridge, still intact at Newtonmore in 1972, also has a curved lattice span, but the whole structure is finer, the latticework being from noticeably thinner material. Note the handsome decorated newel posts and the fact that one set of stairs is reversed to suit this particular location.
Andrew Muckley

Above:
Another curved footbridge, this time of Great Eastern origin, frames two DMUs at Fordham on 16 June 1962. A Derby Lightweight set stands on the left while on the right the 4.21pm to Mildenhall is formed of one of the very distinctive Wickham two-car units. The bridge is similar to the MR pattern, with decorative cast-iron columns supporting the intermediate landings which are illuminated by handsome gas lamps. *L. Sandler*

Above:
A variation on the GER curved footbridge at Stansted station in 1979, shows a deeper lattice section with square columns supporting the left-hand side. Extensions of the vertical frames carry a rather unattractive corrugated iron roof. *Andrew Muckley*

Left:
A very straight version of the GER lattice design is seen here at Long Melford during a local schools activity afternoon in 1961. The bridge has very plain supporting columns and lacks the intermediate landings, producing a very angular structure. It is, however, embellished with the shaped cast-iron beams between the columns, similar to those seen on the Stansted bridge. *John C. Baker*

Left:
A neat angular lattice-girder footbridge served the level crossing and station at Habrough on the Great Central Railway line to Grimsby, seen here in 1985. On the right there are stairs from the road and from the platform, while the left side has only a single staircase. There is an intermediate support under the stairs on the left and intermediate landings on both sides. A plain steel frame supports the structure. *J. Critchley*

Above:
Though the lattice spans are quite plain, just look at the elaborate decoration of the stairs to this Great Northern footbridge at Sandy. Cast columns, newel posts and balustrades are set off by handsome cast gas lamps. This is a 1966 view — doubtless the ECML electrification spelt the end for this bridge, for Sandy station is these days a modern structure. *Andrew Muckley*

Above:
The horizontal lattice-girder footbridge, seen at Duffield station in 1953 was a Midland Railway example on tapered lattice columns. Note that the stairs on the left have an intermediate landing and turn through 180°, back towards the platform. *Ian Allan Library*

Centre right:
The Great Western Railway produced some very fine lattice-girder footbridges, many of which carried their date of construction — usually around the 1880s. This covered example at Culham is typical and shows the rather thick latticework and intermediate landings carried on decorated cast-iron columns. A peaked corrugated iron roof (flat-roofed over the stairs) is carried on a steel framework and has decorative timber valancing. Sadly, few if any of these small footbridges survive intact and the one at Culham has had its roof removed. GWR footbridge kits are available from Hornby (plastic) and a more detailed etched brass kit from Scalelink. *Real Photographs*

Bottom right:
The GWR lattice footbridge at Kemble was originally enclosed with timber screening and glazing like that visible on the left in this view. The bridge here is an integral part of the station buildings, the stairs on either side being built into the structures. Though the side screens have gone, the bridge retains its roof in this 1993 view. *Author*

Above:
An interesting and, probably, interim GWR design is seen at Hungerford station in the 1940s. Though following the general layout of the lattice bridges, this example is of plate-girder construction. It retains the intermediate landing of the earlier type and lacks the glazed draught screens which were frequently found on the plate-girder bridges. I believe this structure still exists, but without its roof, and all other structures at Hungerford have certainly gone. *GWR/Ian Allan Library*

Right:
The GWR introduced this more functional plate-girder footbridge design around 1900 to suit the new 'standard' stations then being built. This example at Cookham shows the features well — a corrugated iron roof, plain plate-girder span, glazed draught screens and much timber construction around the stairs. The decorative valancing under the eaves was retained. The Cookham bridge has gone and the station is reduced to one platform now. *Ian Allan Library*

Below:
Another utilitarian GWR structure was this example adjacent to a level crossing at Thatcham, seen in 1947. A precast concrete span is carried on cast concrete columns which also support concrete stairs. There is a small intermediate landing on each stairway to provide the location for an additional supporting column. The banisters and railings are in 'L'-angle steel bolted to the concrete. *GWR/Ian Allan Library*

Below left:
A really utilitarian footbridge was provided for staff access to the depot at Southall, seen here in the 1950s, with a 'Hall' 4-6-0 passing on a down parcels train. Steel girders support a lightweight steel structure which branches on the right to serve the down side of the station area and (centre) the motive power depot. Note the hoops to retain the structural 'box'-section of the spans. *Ian Allan Library*

Right:
As part of the Clacton/Walton electrification in the 1950s a new footbridge with increased headroom was required at Weeley station. The new concrete bridge is seen here looking very much like a model just standing in place on the platform. It is built entirely of precast concrete components and has an intermediate landing on either side. The raised headroom is obvious when compared to the roadbridge beyond, which probably also needed modification to clear the overhead wires. *BR*

Above:
A view which shows a concrete footbridge under construction at Littlehampton during Southern Railway electrification work in the 1930s. The SR established a concrete works at Exmouth Junction which produced all manner of precast equipment, including lamp posts, concrete fencing and even station nameboards. *BR*

Centre left:
Another example of the Exmouth Junction products is this concrete footbridge at Seaton Junction, seen in 1962. A variety of different components enabled bridges to be built for almost any location. The old Hornby-Dublo range included a metal model of a concrete footbridge which was extremely effective and now commands high prices on the secondhand market. *Ian Allan Library*

Bottom left:
A cast-concrete footbridge of modern, 1980s, construction at Theale, near Reading. Road improvements and station reconstruction are the reasons for this new bridge in dark-coloured concrete with steps and walls cast *in situ. Author*

FUELLING POINTS

DIESEL traction needs far fewer visits to a depot for maintenance than does steam. However, diesels still require fuelling at regular intervals so the advent of diesels brought the need for small areas where fuel could be topped up from adjacent tanks. In some places tanks were provided in steam depots or near to main line stations — sometimes old steam locomotive tenders were used as makeshift fuel bowsers. These days, fuelling points are usually provided at depots, yards and points where staff sign on for duty.

Above:
A simple early-style fuelling point for diesel units is seen here with a railwayman about to top up the tank of a Derby Lightweight DMU. A 5,000gal storage tank is mounted on concrete cradles and carries a steel platform for fuelling from a railway-tank wagon. Fuelling would be by a hose much the same as those found at a petrol station — a typical diesel carries about 150gal of fuel. *Ian Allan Library*

Right:
A major locomotive-fuelling facility of the 1960s is seen here typically located alongside the filth and contamination of the steam-locomotive depot at Leeds Holbeck. A rudimentary shelter is provided for about half-a-dozen fuelling hoses fed from tanks located either underground or elsewhere on the depot site. *Eric Treacy/Millbrook House collection*

Above:
This is the 'supply' end of the fuelling facility at Old Oak Common diesel depot, about 1990. Fuel supplies are delivered by the train of tank wagons and discharged through the flexible hoses into a large tank, on which the photographer is standing. Locomotive fuelling is carried out in a separate shed, off to the right of the picture. *Author*

Right and below:
Two views of the locomotive fuelling point at Peterborough West Yard in 1994. A Class 08 shunter stands alongside the cylindrical fuel tank. The smaller tanks contain lubricating oils, and supplies of antifreeze and degreasants are also maintained on site. *Author*

GOODS SHEDS

FROM the earliest days of railways goods were carried — even before passengers on some lines — and a means of loading and unloading those goods was required. Loading banks or platforms were provided and these were quickly supplied with some sort of cover so that they could be used in all weathers. By the 1840s, on railways such as the Great Western, the goods shed, an enclosed warehouse with unloading platform and crane, had already evolved. As railways developed so the goods shed became larger and more sophisticated and in major cities warehouses were provided where whole trains could be loaded or unloaded under cover and where road vehicles could be brought inside to be loaded direct from the railway wagon. From the 1930s to the 1950s the use of such depots was at its peak with millions of tons of 'sundries' traffic, but after that, wagonload traffic declined in favour of road transport until today there is virtually nothing other than bulk traffic being moved by BR.

Below:
The very simple goods shed at Wotton on the Metropolitan Great Central Joint Line is seen in 1935. The short platform can accommodate only a couple of wagons of goods to be transhipped across to road transport under the protection of a rudimentary wooden awning. *LGRP/Real Photographs*

Left:
A substantial goods shed for a minor railway was this example at Lynton on the narrow gauge Lynton & Barnstaple Railway. Built of local stone, it contained a single siding, an unloading platform and two bays for road vehicles, protected by wooden awnings. It is seen here after closure by the Southern Railway in 1935, and the structure survives today having been converted into two cottages. *Real Photographs*

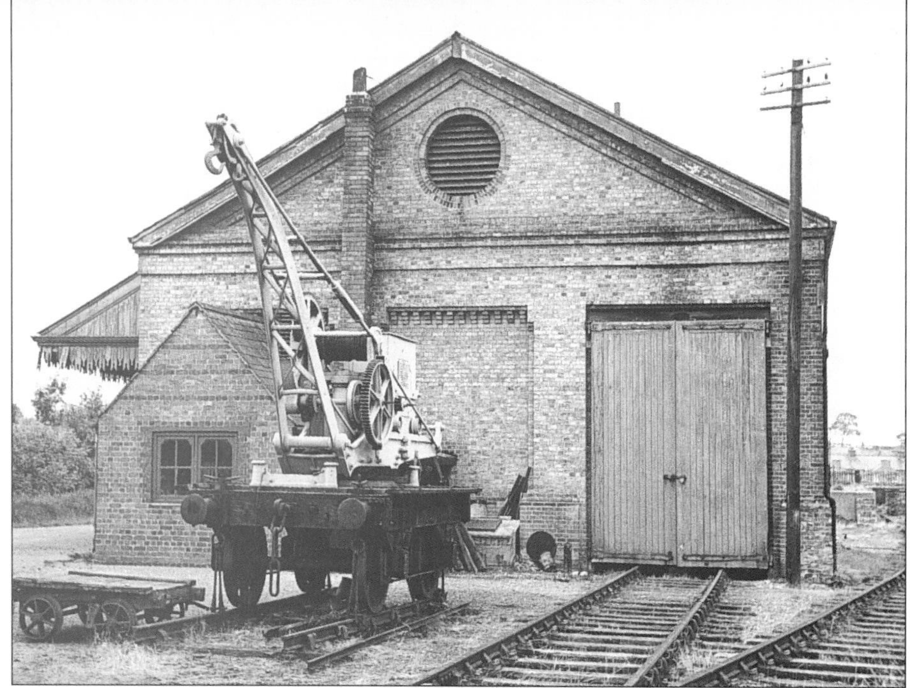

Left:
A more substantial brick-built goods shed is seen here at Olney on the former Midland Railway line from Northampton to Bedford. Doors are provided for security, and the road loading bays on the left have wooden awnings. A small goods office is also provided and, for the largest loads, an elderly hand-operated crane has been strategically placed adjacent to the shed. *Andrew Muckley*

Centre left:
Seen from the train in May 1962 is the small timber goods shed at Bourton-on-the-Water. Again the 'standard' configuration for a rural goods shed accommodates a single siding, this time with the roof extended to protect the road loading bays, and a lean-to goods office is attached to one end. In the right foreground is the separate cattle loading dock, by this time out of use. *Ian Allan Library*

Below:
The Oxford, Worcester & Wolverhampton Railway provided some very substantial timber goods sheds at its rural stations, and several lasted into the 1960s. These sheds were distinctive in having two parallel entrances: one road and the other rail, either side of a central platform. In this view at Chipping Campden the hand-operated derrick can be glimpsed through the nearer doorway, which is wider than necessary for a single siding because it originally accommodated Brunel's 7ft broad gauge. *Author's collection*

Above:
This view of the small goods shed at Eardisley, on the former Midland Railway Hereford–Three Cocks line, is useful in that it shows some of the other features of a typical rural goods yard. The pick-up freight is present, along with a couple of lorries and in the foreground is the road weighbridge with its steel platform and adjacent office. Even in preservation, such items are now rare and I know of no preserved railway which has an operational weighbridge and certainly none which uses its goods shed for its intended purpose. *B. J. Ashworth*

Left:
Closed up and trackless, the goods shed at Nairn, Highland Railway, still survived in 1992. Built of timber and roofed with corrugated iron, it would make an ideal small model. *Author*

Above:
Long disused for railway purposes, the goods shed at Cowbit on the Great Northern & Great Eastern joint line near Spalding was still standing in 1994. The red-brick building, under a slate roof, accommodates one siding and has two road loading bays with green-painted timber doors. *Author*

Centre right:
The stone-built goods shed at St Ives, Cornwall, is not unlike the 4mm scale plastic kit produced by Ratio Models. The shed served a single siding and had sliding doors across both entrance and exit from the siding and the single-road loading bay. The shed was demolished in about 1966. *Author*

Bottom right:
In later years, particularly after World War 2, accommodation at some rural goods yards was expanded with the construction of the so-called 'provender store' for agricultural material, particularly farm feeds and fertilizers. This example at Ross-on-Wye is built of corrugated iron with an asbestos roof. The platform is of concrete slabs on block-built piers. *M. E. M. Lloyd*

Left:
A more familiar provender store is the standard BR version in precast concrete sections and this is a view of the prototype for a design which appeared all over the UK. A splendid model of this type is produced as a plastic kit by Ratio. Like the real thing, the kits can be joined together and adapted to suit larger installations. *BR*

Below:
Now we turn our attention to the larger freight depots provided at major railway centres. These were essentially giant warehouses with loading platforms serving a number of sidings and with totally covered road access. This interior view of the modernised terminal at Huskisson, Liverpool, shows sundries being loaded from a platform-length conveyor belt. *BR*

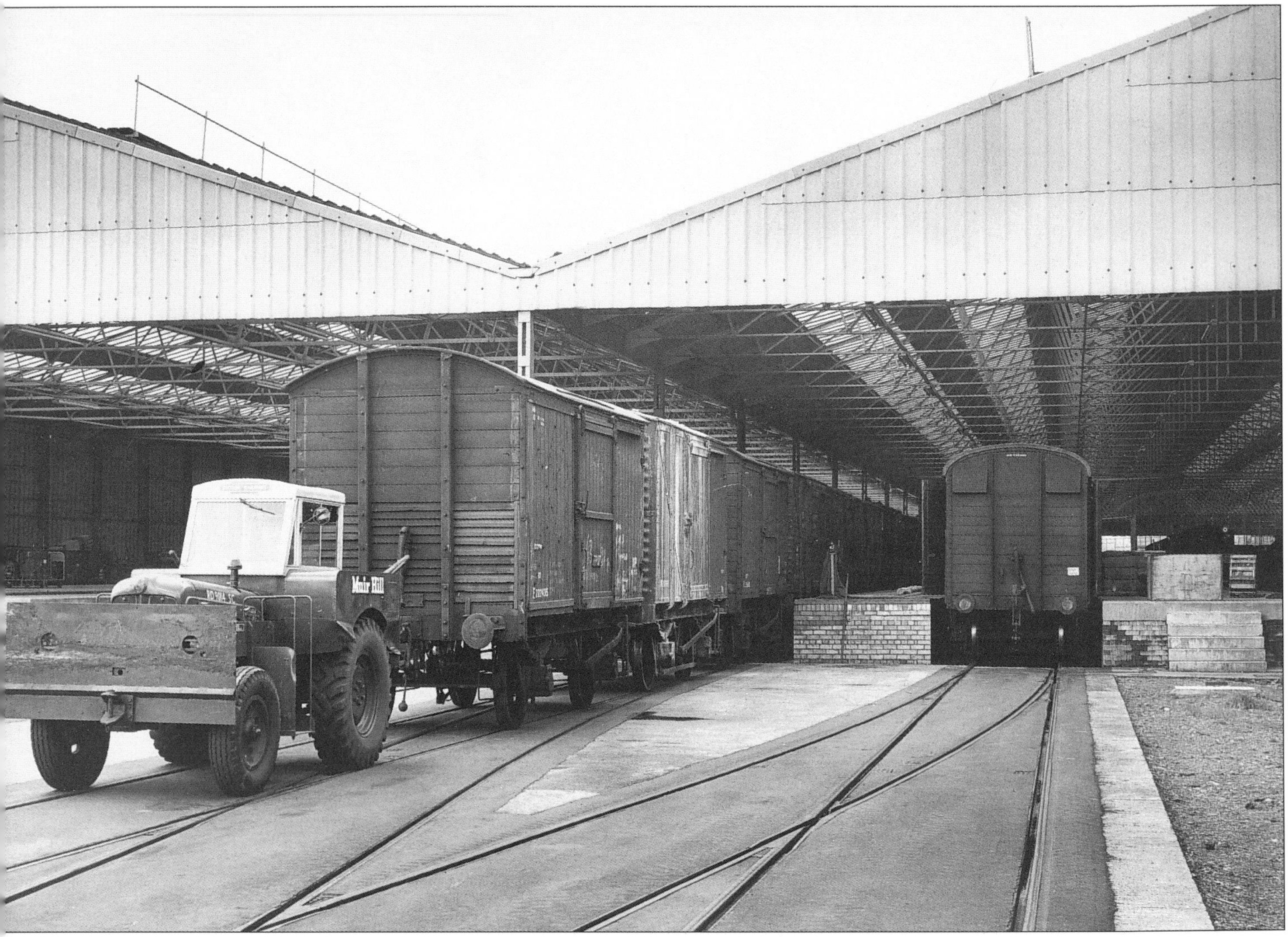
Muir Hill

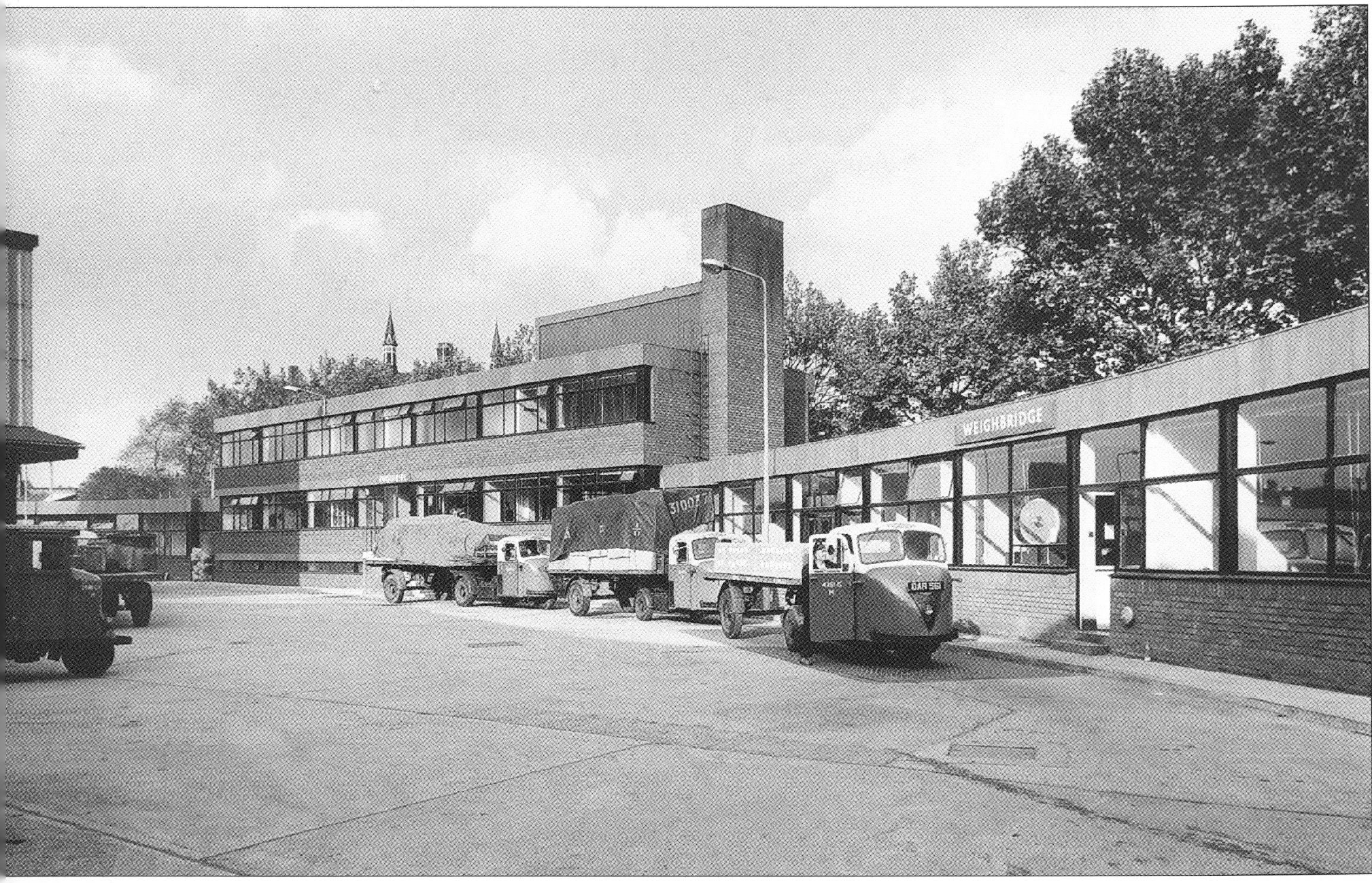
WEIGHBRIDGE
310037
4351 G
M
OAR 561

Above left:
Concrete aprons enclose the rails at Sighthill depot in Scotland in this 1962 view, to enable goods to be shunted by a modified farm tractor. A steel-framed warehouse covers the loading bays. *BR*

Below left:
A 1950s view of a modern freight terminal from the road approach, showing the offices and the weighbridge with Scammell 'mechanical horses' awaiting weighing. *BR*

Above:
The modern brick-built offices of the Tyneside Central Freight Depot at Gateshead seen when new in 1963. *BR*

Centre right:
The road side of the Sheffield freight terminal in September 1965 showing the parking area for loading trailers. *BR*

Bottom right:
The modestly-sized modern freight terminal at Stockton-on-Tees, seen in 1960. The brick and concrete structure, with glazed roof, covers some four sidings and has road access rather than platforms between them. *BR*

Below:
Inside the Stockton terminal from the same era as the picture of the terminal on the previous page, loaded trailers wait in marked bays with goods for distribution throughout the area. Even individual factory customers have marked bays. *BR*

Right:
By the 1970s the emphasis had moved away from general freight and the only sundries traffic on the railway was being dealt with by the Rail Express Parcels section. These trains operated between major terminals with road delivery onwards to the customer. One such new major terminal was provided at Peterborough and is seen here with the corporate image signposting of the day, in July 1970. *BR*

Below right:
One of the last attempts to keep the Speedlink wagonload traffic alive was the encouragement of private-enterprise rail terminals served by complete freight trains made up of varied wagons with loads for different customers. The idea was that those customers would then collect their freight, by road, from the rail terminal. One such enterprise was known originally as 'Didcot Inland Port', opened as the Milton Freight Terminal. The main transit shed, with one siding, extensive storage and a large road loading bay, is seen here nearing completion in June 1981. The Speedlink service was withdrawn a few years later, and all wagonload traffic on BR then ceased. *BR*

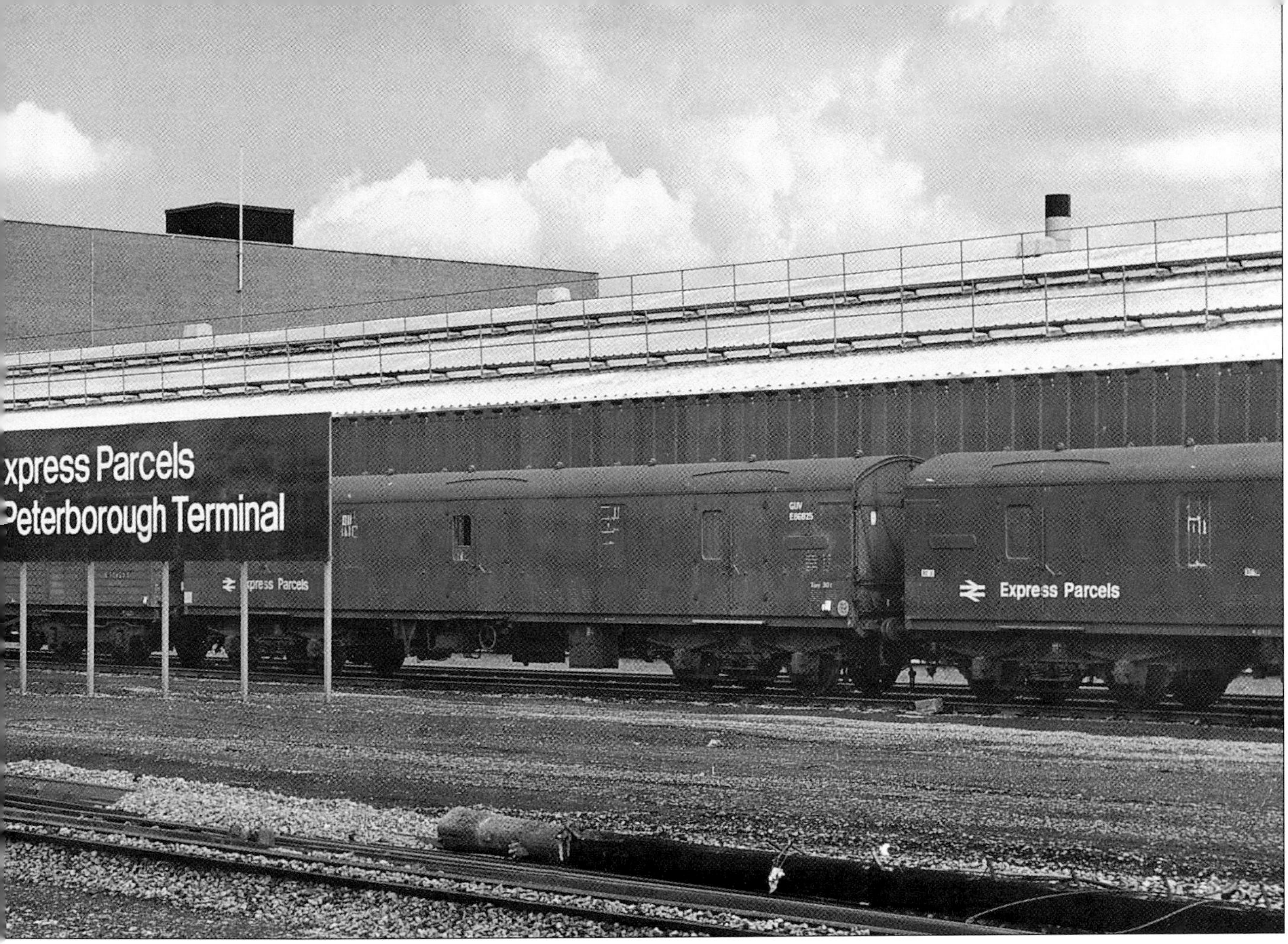

xpress Parcels
Peterborough Terminal
Express Parcels

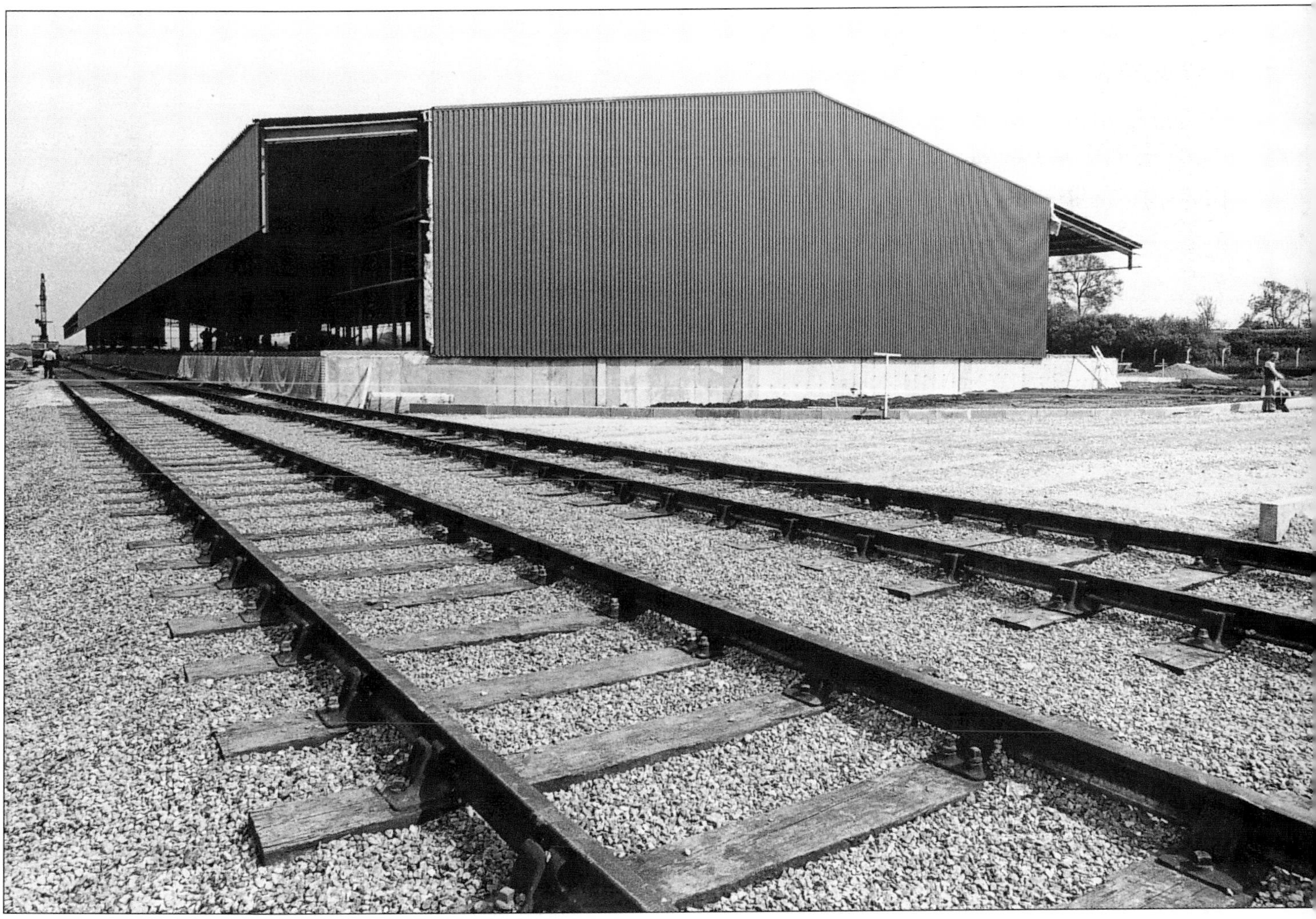

GROUND FRAMES

GROUND frames are groups of signal or point levers not installed in a signalbox but operated at ground level either in the open or from a rudimentary shelter or hut.

Left:
The ground frame at Furze Platt halt near Maidenhead was operated by the porter/signalman in charge of the adjacent halt. The five levers controlled signals protecting the level crossing. *Ian Allan Library*

Above:
A Class 31 diesel leaves the yard at Braintree on 5 August 1971. The points are controlled by the ground frame, unlocked by the Annetts key which the shunter is holding. Instruments in the little cabin provide communication with the station signalbox, 1/4 mile away. *G. R. Mortimer*

Below:
The ground frame at Millbrook station on the former London & North Western line from Bletchley to Bedford, seen in 1994. The 11-lever frame controls signals protecting the level crossing and is mounted under a rudimentary corrugated iron roof decorated with the wheeltrims which have presumably fallen off passing cars as they negotiated the level crossing. Note the modern non-slip surface in front of the ground frame! *Author*

GROUNDED BODIES

ONE of the fascinating features of the 1960s railway scene was being able to find the bodies of ancient railway carriages and wagons in use as offices, messrooms and bothies. The vehicle bodies were usually taken off their underframes and grounded or supported on bases of blocks or old sleepers.

Above:
On the up platform at Shipton-for-Burford station stands an old GWR carriage body from a four- or six-wheeled vehicle of 19th century origin. The Oxford–Worcester line was littered with such vehicles into the 1960s. *Real Photographs*

Left:
A grounded van body supported on old sleepers provides additional storage beside the goods depot at Calne station in 1965. *Author*

HALTS

THE Great Western Railway is best known for the use of halts — small (usually unstaffed) stations serving minor points of population with little more than a railway 'bus stop' facility. The GWR began introducing them in the early years of the present century in order to increase receipts on lightly used lines in rural areas. Their use spread to urban areas and they were, eventually, found on lines throughout the UK.

Above:
A typical GWR halt style represented by Poyle halt which served the village of Stanwell Moor, two miles distant. A timber shelter with corrugated iron roof stands on a platform of ash faced with stout timbers. This halt lasted until 1965 although the shelter burned down two years earlier. The site is now almost under the M25.
Author's collection

Left:
The archetypal GWR halt was as seen here at Mithian on the branch to Newquay in Cornwall. The platform is brick but would more usually have been timber or even ash. The shelter is a corrugated 'pagoda' of the type built by Joseph Ash & Sons of Birmingham and widely used by the GWR as shelters and cycle sheds. Oil lamps are provided at this remote location, seen probably in the 1920s. *Real Photographs*

Left:
The halt at Quintrell Downs on the Newquay branch retained its slightly larger than usual corrugated iron waiting room in the late 1980s when this view was taken. The platform is brick-faced and there was a hand-operated gated level crossing here until its replacement by an 'open' crossing with warning lights. *Author*

Centre left:
Halt construction continued right into the 1960s when concrete structures like this example at Poyle Estate, near Colnbrook, were erected. Made of precast components, it served an industrial development but its service was withdrawn in March 1965. *Author*

Below:
Another tiny BR-era halt dating from 1959 was Troublehouse, on the Tetbury branch, built to serve a public house and opened in conjunction with the introduction of diesel railbus services. Another was provided at Church's Hill and two more on the adjacent Cirencester branch. The low platforms were reached by folding steps fitted on the railbus. Both branches were closed in early April 1964. *Michael Farr*

LAMPS (Station)

THIS section illustrates just a small selection from the wealth of variety which has existed in station lamps of oil, gas and electric types. The lamp posts have comprised timber, cast-iron, concrete, and recently tubular steel, and have also reflected the design influences of their era. Remarkably, despite the almost total standardisation of some station furniture, such as seats, the electric lamp post still reflects nearly as much variety of design as did its gas predecessor.

Above:
Standard 4-6-0 No 73102 draws up to the platform at Kilbirnie with a Glasgow–Ardrossan train in 1959. The platform boasts a row of fine lantern-top gas lamps with cast-iron posts, flared at the base. This was a joint Caledonian and Glasgow & South Western station, and the lamps probably date from before 1923. *G. H. Robin*

Left:
A derelict oil lamp at Gatehouse of Fleet station on the Portpatrick & Wigtownshire Joint line, seen in July 1964. Such relics abounded throughout the system in the 1960s, but were quickly swept away with the onset of closures and modernisation. The lantern top, once glazed, would have housed a removable oil lamp and reflector. The post, in this instance, is a length of bullhead rail, crimped at the top to accept the collar on which the lantern is mounted. *R. H. Short*

Left:
This fine gas lantern at Witney, Oxfordshire, was suspended from the waiting shelter roof by nothing more than the 1in gas pipe — it certainly would not be allowed on today's safety-conscious railway! The square lantern is equipped with a broad hood to reflect the light downwards. The rocking lever which operated the gas supply can be seen above the hood, with cords attached to either end. *Ian Allan Library*

Above:
An example of a preserved station, County School in Norfolk, equipped with replica lamps fitted with low-energy electric bulbs to give an impression of gas lighting. The cast-iron column has 'arms' to support the lamplighter's ladder. *Author*

Left:
A restored lantern-top oil lamp at Staverton Bridge station shows a typical GWR cast-iron post, of a type used for oil and gas lamps. The front glass carries the station name, also a common practice for oil and gas lamps. *R. Price*

Left:
The column of this GWR lamp is the same as the oil version at Staverton Bridge, but this example (at Brixham in 1961) is fitted with a standard GWR gas top. The scroll-shaped supporting pipe arrangement is generally known as a 'half-harp' — there were full harps too, though much less common. This pattern of gas lamp was widely used by the GWR and even at stations such as Oxford they lasted until at least the late 1960s. *Ian Allan Library*

Right:
A later style of GWR gas (or sometimes electric) lamp is seen here disused at Staines West station in 1965. The tapered and fluted cast-iron column carries a swan-neck pipe supporting a simple enamelled 'dish' shade. Stationmaster Tom Bye is approaching with a step ladder to remove one of the totem signs which the author had just bought for the princely sum of 15s (75p). Pity I did not buy the whole lamp post! *Author*

Above:
Yet another style of GWR gas lamp was this very plain version with two slender pipes supporting a very flat reflector and gas top. The post is cast-iron and the curious broad bases were apparently unique to Pwllheli. Usually, this type of gas top was mounted on the style of post shown at Staverton Bridge and Brixham in earlier illustrations. A 1972 view. *G. S. Cocks*

Above left:
A swan-neck gas lamp installation by the LNER seen at Haverhill in February 1967. The short cast-iron post is mounted on a brick wall. The advent of swan-neck lamps meant that station names on the glass were no longer practical and so the lamp-tablet enamelled sign appeared. In BR days lamp-tablets were often replaced by the familiar BR totems like the one seen here, which would have been in Eastern Region dark blue. *G. R. Mortimer*

Above right:
The Southern Railway's swan-neck gas lamp was a handsome affair — possibly inherited from the London & South Western. This example at Barnstaple Junction has the barley-twist cast-iron post with arms, and an SR lamp-tablet sign. *Ian Allan Library*

Left:
The most familiar of Southern Railway lamps was the concrete post electric variety as seen here at Virginia Water, complete with its hexagonal opal glass shade and an SR lamp-tablet sign. In some instances the glass shade was replaced by an enamelled 'dish' shade and this version is available in model form in 4mm scale from Chris Leigh. *Author*

Above:
Now we come to the 'modern' electric lamps. The use of fluorescent tubes revived the opportunity to display station names on the glass, as here at Harlow Town in 1960. The post is a tapered square precast concrete design, considered stylish and modern in its day. *BR*

Right:
A different style of short fluorescent fitting is seen on these modern concrete posts at Handforth on the London Midland Region in the 1960s. These thick concrete castings are much less attractive and the BR totem sign is still obligatory. *BR*

Left:
Lamps similar to those at Harlow were photographed in 1954 in a night-time view of Twickenham, a showpiece station rebuild of the period. *General Electric*

Centre left:
The 1970s saw the emergence of the tubular steel lamp post in this version which was almost a BR standard design. The small fluorescent top was angled upwards and at the base of the post was a pivot arrangement which allowed the whole post to be dropped down horizontally for maintenance. This was a 1983 view at Settle station. *Brian Morrison*

Bottom left:
A similar style of tubular steel post is seen here at Ystrad Mynach station in 1975, but this time fitted with a conventional bulb top. *BR*

Top right:
This 1990s view of Kemble station shows the more recent style of tubular metal post and fluorescent head. A distinctive feature is the narrow web where the head and post join. This design is particularly simple and elegant and replaced a much less attractive 1960s installation at Kemble. *Author*

Right:
Another very modern style is this large fluorescent head fitted to a tubular steel post and is seen at Lowestoft in 1994. The pivot at the base of the post can be clearly seen in this view. *Author*

Far right:
Yet another modern variant on the pivoted tubular post is this lofty round-topped design employed on the Regional Railways station at Oulton Broad North in East Anglia. *Author*

Lowestoft

Oulton
Broad North

LOADING GAUGES

WHEN the railways had common carrier status they were obliged to accept a wide variety of cargoes, some of which were large and bulky items. An essential feature of almost every goods yard was the loading gauge, a simple device which enabled staff to ensure that large loads would fit within the 'loading gauge' of the railway — that is, they would pass under bridges and not strike over-line equipment or passing trains.

Left:
The loading gauge in its simplest form comprised a gibbet post from which a metal arc-shape was suspended on chains. If the load struck the metal arc it was too high and therefore 'out of gauge'. This fine example at Brackley Central, on the Great Central line in 1966, has the refinement of hinged outer ends to the arc which can be lowered by means of a chain. *Andrew Muckley*

Above:
An ancient view of the London & North Western Railway yard at Willesden shows a timber frame carrying the rather rudimentary loading gauges, but doubtless they were just as effective.
LPC Collection/Ian Allan Ltd

Right:
In this view the siding has gone but the loading gauge still stands — temporarily. A concrete post and steel arm support this loading gauge on the North Eastern Railway line at Alston. *Ian Allan Library*

MAIL COLLECTION APPARATUS (TPO)

THE practice of picking up and setting down mail bags from nonstop mail trains was widely used on BR main lines and ceased only when the better acceleration of diesel and electric traction enabled station stops to be made without adversely affecting transit times.

The Travelling Post Office (TPO) apparatus at the lineside consisted of a net for collecting the mailbags and a gantry arrangement, known as a traductor arm, from which the moving train snatched the bags into a net on the carriage side as it passed. In 4mm scale, both Hornby-Dublo and the present Hornby Railways have produced their own operating TPO coach and lineside equipment. Some very fine, non-operating TPO coach models are produced in 4mm scale by Southern Pride Models.

Below:
The distinctive chequerboard pattern indicated to the TPO train crew the precise position of the lineside apparatus so that the traductor arms and net on the carriage could be swung out in readiness. This example was near Maidenhead. *D. B. Hart*

Right:
The lineside TPO equipment at Maidenhead. The mail bags, placed in leather pouches, would be suspended from the traductor arm which would then be swung round towards the track. As the carriage passed and its net snatched the pouches, so its own pouches would be deposited into the lineside net. *D. B. Hart*

Left:
Mail pouches are placed in position on the traductor arms of an installation on the LMR West Coast main line in July 1954. The man on the left is attaching steadying cords to the pouches to prevent them moving unduly in the draught of the passing train.
R. E. Vincent

Below:
The Great Western Railway stables at Chipping Norton station, seen in the 1970s when derelict, still show how they were converted with a pair of end doors to house the local delivery lorry. *Author*

MOTOR LORRY FACILITIES

FOR many years this century horses and motor lorries were interchangeable for deliveries from railway goods yards to local businesses. Gradually the motor lorry took over, due in no small measure to the introduction by Scammell of a special three-wheeled tractor and articulated trailer which became known as the 'mechanical horse'. In some rural goods yards the stables were actually converted to house the delivery lorry. (See also the **Goods Sheds** section relating to modern goods facilities.)

PERMANENT WAY

(see Track)

PITS (Inspection)

INSPECTION pits were provided in depots for the servicing of steam and diesel traction. They are still an essential feature of locomotive maintenance facilities, large and small.

PLATELAYERS' HUTS

FOR the gangers — the men who maintained the track — it was essential to provide a shed for storage of tools and equipment and a place where they could take shelter and 'brew up'. Platelayers' huts were usually rudimentary affairs assembled from old sleepers, often with a crude brick chimney so that the men could light a fire to keep warm or brew their tea on. In more enlightened times, the huts have improved and the modern railway has portable buildings or uses converted signalboxes or other redundant structures. The Southern Railway produced a sectional concrete platelayers' hut to a standard design, cast at the company's Exmouth concrete works, and many of these still survive since they are virtually indestructible. Roxey Mouldings produces a 4mm-scale kit for one of the SR type. Timber huts are included in the Wills, Ratio and Merit ranges, all in 4mm scale.

Left:
Brick-built under a pantile roof, this little platelayers' hut at Staines West was a substantial affair which survived long after the goods yard was turned over to other uses, and it is here seen marooned inside the oil depot. It was demolished soon after this 1980s view. *Author*

Below:
Old sleepers have certainly been used for the older part of this hut at Shipton for Burford station on the Oxford–Worcester Line, though a newer section has also been added, leaving the one-time external brick chimney in the middle of the structure. In the foreground is the almost obligatory hand-operated grindstone. This was used for sharpening tools, particularly the scythes used for cutting lineside vegetation in the steam era. *Author*

Left:
A view of the modern concrete-lined inspection pit inside Feltham diesel depot in 1966. The pit contains fluorescent lighting and recessed heating pipes. An 0-6-0 diesel shunter stands over the pit. Feltham depot was later closed. *BR*

Left:
To the right of 'Small Prairie' No 4567 is the platelayers' hut at Black Dog halt, seen in 1962. It is built of vertical timbers — probably old sleepers — with a wooden door and a corrugated iron roof. *Don Lovelock*

PLATFORM BARROWS

(see Trolleys)

PLATFORMS (Station)

OWING to the design of British railway carriages (based originally on the horse-drawn coach) with their floor height some 4ft from ground level, it has always been necessary to provide platforms to enable passengers to board and alight easily. The North American and Continental practice of providing end platforms and steps on the carriages was never widely used in this country and restricted to a few light railways. These days, in order to comply with regulations regarding disabled access and public safety, platform heights and lengths are stringently regulated. However, on parts of the main line railway system, platforms well below standard height can still be found. These were often inherited from minor railway companies of the Victorian era, amongst whom there were wide variations in platform dimensions.

Left:
Stewartby, on the Bedford– Bletchley line, reflects the modern style of platform construction, using cylindrical concrete piles to support wooden beams which carry the timber platform surface. The platform has a wooden fence and modern Network SouthEast lighting and seats. Photographed July 1994. *Author*

Right:
Here's a splendid example of a lower-than-standard platform, dating from the original 19th century construction of the line and still in use in 1994. The wooden step provided at Millbrook, near Bedford, shows just how low the platform is. It has brick parapet walls and is surfaced with brick paviors, only the edging being concrete blocks. Recent Health & Safety stipulations about platforms have thrown the future of such stations into grave doubt since the traffic levels at places such as Millbrook are insufficient to justify the huge cost of rebuilding to the new specifications. One wonders whether anyone has ever suffered injury at Millbrook because of the low platform. Other points to note in this July 1994 view are the original timber waiting shelter and the hand-operated metal gates to the level crossing. *Author*

Above:
A modern installation dating from the mid-1980s is Crossflatts, near Bingley in West Yorkshire. The structure here has timber-surfaced platforms on concrete footings, but with small brick-built waiting shelters. *BR*

Above:
A 1950s view which shows platform lengthening work at Billericay in order to accommodate 12-car trains. The platform extension employs standard precast concrete components. *BR*

Centre left:
A splendid August 1952 view at Elsenham station, erstwhile Great Eastern Railway, in which the rear coach of the Thaxted branch train shows the very low platform height on this light railway line. The coach has extra steps to suit the branch platforms. The platform surface is tarmac and spotlessly maintained. *R. E. Vincent*

Bottom left:
Surely one of the smallest platforms on BR, Mill Road was a halt on the Elsenham & Thaxted branch. Stout timbers face a small earth mound and the lamp and two signs seem to fill the platform's entire length. *W. S. Garth*

Right:
A stoutly constructed wooden platform of conventional height but very short, this is Dee Street halt, Banchory, in May 1970. Note the Tilley oil lamp post with its metal frame and simple wooden step for the lampman. *Andrew Muckley*

Below:
The stone-built platform of the goods siding at Black Dog halt, near Calne, seen in the 1950s. The construction contrasts with the brick-faced platform of the halt itself, on the left.
Don Lovelock

Above:
Once surmounted by a substantial station building, this is one of the staggered platforms at Whittlesey station seen in 1994. A former Great Eastern Railway station, the platform is still the original though it has been resurfaced and new fencing has been erected. *Author*

Below:
The timber-framed platform of the Great Western halt at Furze Platt near Maidenhead is seen in this 1960s view. The fenceposts and lamp posts are concrete though the rest of the structure is timber throughout. In 4mm scale a plastic kit for a timber-framed platform is available in the Wills range. *Ian Allan Library*

POSTER BOARDS

ADVERTISEMENT displays have long been an essential part of the railway station scene, enabling the railway company to display essential information, promote its own services and obtain revenue by renting space to outside advertisers. Today, with many stations now unstaffed, the display of information has become more vital than ever and standard display boards have been produced.

Above:
The modern standard poster display board as used by Regional Railways at many of its stations. This display is typical but it could be just two standard-sized boards or as many as six in one unit. Oulton Broad South, 1994. A 4mm-scale casting of this board is produced by Chris Leigh.
Author

PRIVATE SIDINGS (Petroleum Products)

BLOCK trains of petroleum products, including central-heating fuel, tar, creosote, petrol and aviation fuel, are still very much a part of the railway scene. Some of the discharge installations are quite small and would provide an interesting feature for a model railway.

Above:
Private sidings are usually fenced and separated from the rest of the railway system by gates. This single siding serving a depot for central-heating fuel was installed in the mid-1960s. *Author*

Left:
A similar viewpoint to the previous picture, this view shows the discharge pipes for unloading the wagons, the storage tanks (left) and the loading shed for road vehicles (centre). *Author*

Above:
Discharge pipes unloading a Shell Mex-BP train in the siding at Banbury station. The storage tank can be seen on the right. *BR*

Below:
Fuel storage tanks in this factory adjacent to the Bedford–Bletchley line are actually made from old railway tank wagons and still carry their original numbers. The tank on the right reveals the fixings for its oval 'Esso' placard, thus suggesting a perfect use for three Dapol Esso tank wagon kits. *Author*

Left:
Squeezed between industrial buildings at the former Colnbrook station site is the discharge point for tankers of aviation fuel. There is no visible storage facility here, the fuel being pumped through underground pipes to the 'tank farm' at Heathrow Airport, thus suggesting another possibility for a model installation in quite a small space. *Author*

SAND DRAGS

THE sand drag is a means of slowing down and stopping runaway vehicles and although sand drags were never common, they certainly make for an interesting feature. They would be provided where a siding or secondary line ran downhill to a junction and a means of protecting the junction from runaways was required. A catch point (see section named **Catch Points**) would be used to divert the runaway onto the sand drag, which would consist of either a long pit filled with sand or, as in the example illustrated, two sand-filled metal troughs.

Left:
At Welford Park on the Newbury–Lambourn branch a United States Air Force stores complex was served by rail. The branch is seen here on the left, with the connection to the USAF base (otherwise known as RAF Welford) on the right. The base siding rises steeply towards the camera and to protect the exchange sidings in the centre a sand drag is provided. This sand drag is actually interlaced with the running line, the sand being contained in metal troughing mounted on the sleepers. The arrangement is unusually long, but one suspects that, with wagons of explosives being handled here, every possible precaution had to be taken. In such circumstances it would be important not only to stop the runaway vehicles, but to ensure that they remained upright and suffered minimal damage. *Author*

SEATS (Station)

STATION seats came in wide variety, often being designed as a distinctive feature of the owning railway, the company crest or initials displayed in the cast-iron ends. These seats disappeared in vast numbers during the 1960s, but the Great Western, at least, had produced so many that they still survive at some stations today. More recently, however, station seats have been a target of vandalism and have even been thrown on to the track, so a modern vandal-resistant design has been produced. This seat, entirely produced from metal, is cold and not very comfortable, but is able to be firmly fixed into the platform surface.

Above:
The classic Victorian bench seat had cast-iron decorative ends and timber slats. The most expensive examples contained elaborate designs within the cast legs and examples appeared as park benches and as deckchairs on ships (the *Titanic*, for instance, boasted a splendid design). These examples at Perth in the 1960s have cast ends including armrests with the initials of the Caledonian Railway incorporated. The scroll shape of the slatted seat might not have been very comfortable. *G. P. Stilley*

Left:
A much simpler scroll shape was produced in wrought iron by the South Eastern Railway, with a separate casting of the initials bolted into the leg unit. The top slat has a recess for the station name, either as cast letters or as an enamelled metal plate. These seats got moved around during their career, hence this one at New Romney in March 1964 has lost its name. I remember one which resided into the 1970s at Feltham — miles from SER territory! *G. Boyes*

Above:
The well-known GWR-type seat with 'scroll' initials as seen here in the 1960s was the earliest of three Swindon patterns which varied only in the style of initials. A longer version than this, with a third central cast frame, was more common.
Author's collection

Right:
Another familiar GWR-seat style was this version of the cast frame introduced with the 'shirt-button' logo of the 1930s. There was also another variation of the scroll lettering (only one known example, at Kemble) and a post-1948 version with the letters 'BR (W)' on the solid roundel. *T. G. Flinders*

Below:
The beautiful station garden at Verney Junction in July 1966 includes statuettes, a pond and a scroll-shaped bench seat with simple wrought-iron ends. *Andrew Muckley*

Left:
Seats similar to the one at Verney Junction, and of LMS origin, adorn the immaculate new platforms at the rebuilt Coventry station in the 1950s. They look out of place among all that clinical concrete and tubular steel. *BR*

Below:
The Midland Railway and other LMS constituents were among the users of this 'rustic' seat style which was probably a readily available commercial product since it cropped up in so many varied locations. Cast-iron leg and armrest units are designed to look like tree branches — a different 'arm-less' casting is used in the centre. *D. Smith*

Left:
The standard modern all-steel seat is designed to resist vandalism — there's no wood to carve or break, the perforated surface doesn't attract graffiti, and the seat can be firmly anchored into the platform surface. The same style has been used by Network SouthEast, Regional Railways and various municipal authorities. This one was at Whittlesey in 1994. *Author*

SIGNALBOXES (Manual)

THE existence of numerous railway designs together with those of several private contractors meant that BR inherited thousands of signalboxes of widely differing architectural style and with very different equipment. In the past 30 years the spread of multiple-aspect colour light signalling (MAS) has spelled the end for most of these old manual signalboxes, yet a few survive, either in pockets of semaphore signalling, or as locations for closed circuit TV control of level crossings. Others have been converted for uses outside signalling or have been lovingly restored by preservation societies, often using parts of several demolished signalboxes to make one good one.

Left:
The family likeness of Great Eastern Railway signalboxes is easy to see from these five illustrations. Timber signalboxes were widely used by most railway companies in areas where ground stability was bad and deep foundations would be required for brick-built structures. Thus, with much of the fenland area of East Anglia being very soft, the GER found timber 'boxes were ideal and used them almost exclusively. This small structure with external steps and a simple front landing survives as the control centre for the swing bridge at Oulton Broad. A 1994 picture. *Author*

Below left:
A larger structure in similar style is found at Oulton Broad North station where it controls the adjacent level crossing. The locking room windows with eight panes and operating windows with nine panes are a distinctive feature, as are the shallow-pitched slate roof and end nameboards. This is also a 1994 view. *Author*

Top:
The windows, roof and landing and other essential features are the same, but the GER signalbox at Whittlesey required a higher vantage point for the operating floor to provide a view over the extensive yards which once surrounded it, and to the station some distance away. It was still in use in summer 1994. *Author*

Above:
Another GER example, again without a front landing, is this 'box photographed in 1993 at Downham Market where it controls the adjacent level crossing. The windows here are a modified design with narrow vertical panes. *Author*

Below:
A slightly taller than standard GER 'box was provided with a loftier location by mounting it on the platform at Yaxham station. This location did not require a front landing and the style of the upper windows, with only eight panes, is different. Yaxham is on the Wymondham–Dereham line and currently the subject of a preservation project.
Ian Allan Library

Right:
The London & North Western Railway generally employed a brick-built base with timber for the operating level on its small and medium sized 'boxes. This preserved example at Wansford is typical of a medium-sized installation and it also controls the gated level crossing. *Author*

Below:
This small platform-mounted signalbox at Portsmouth Arms in North Devon is an early LSWR design with timber operating floor section on top of a stone base. The hipped slate roof and lean-to porch are distinctive features. This was a 1962 view. *Author's collection*

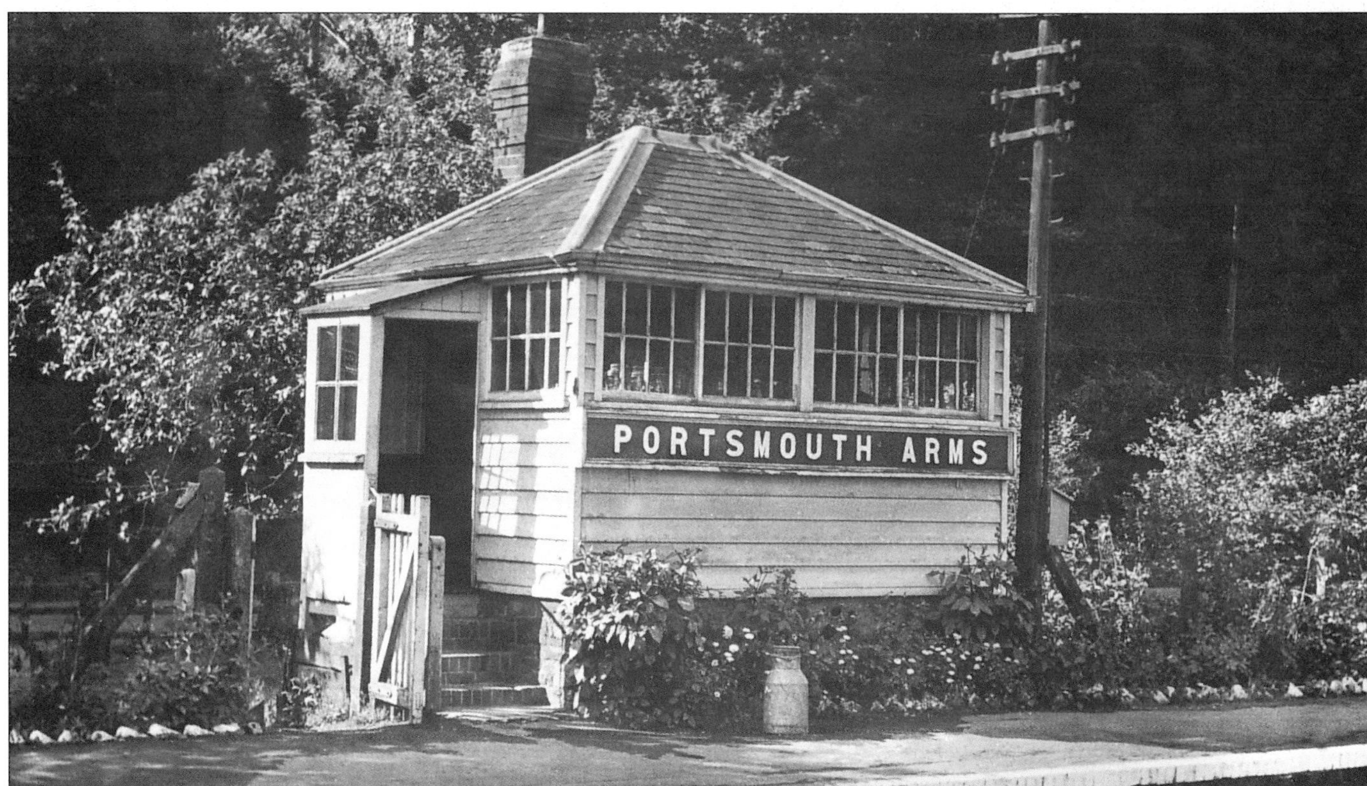

Right:
Family likeness to the LSWR signalbox at Portsmouth Arms is obvious in this view of the 19th century LSWR 'box at Instow, seen here in the late 1970s. As this 'box is more normally located than in the previous picture, controlling a level crossing and station area, the stone base housing the locking frame is somewhat deeper. The woodwork, roof and porch are almost identical to Portsmouth Arms, and there were many other similar 'boxes (at Lapford, for instance). Instow signalbox is a 'listed' building and has since been restored, with crossing gates and a short length of track outside, by the Bideford & Instow Railway Group. *Author*

Right:
For larger signalboxes, and in more urban areas, a later style of LSWR signalbox was equally distinctive. This example at Virginia Water station is typical and shows the salient features: hipped slate roof with distinctive vents, operating room windows with curved tops to the upper panes and the brickwork carried up to roof level in the centre of the front elevation. This 'box, with wooden steps and outside porch, succumbed with the Feltham resignalling, although it did remain standing until the station was rebuilt some years later. *Author*

Above:
The LSWR signalbox at Pooley Green controlled only the adjacent level crossing and was demolished when automatic half-barriers were installed in 1976. Basic features are the same as Virginia Water, though it is too small to require the full-height brickwork at the front. *Author*

Right:
A contrasting Southern signalbox in the shape of the London, Brighton & South Coast Railway example at Midhurst. Numerous sliding casements are provided at operating level, with herring-bone-pattern woodwork beneath them. The 'box was situated at the top of an embankment, so wood construction is used throughout. *Real Photographs*

Above:
A platform-mounted early Great Western Railway signalbox at Halesowen, seen in October 1966. The wooden operating floor is elevated above the platform on eight courses of engineering bricks. The outlet for the rodding and signal wires can be seen in the front of the platform. There are very small locking room windows in the brickwork, and a short staircase to the outside landing at the far end. *Author*

Left:
Cookham signalbox was a substantial brick-built example of a standard GWR design featuring large windows which give plenty of light to the operating floor. Arched locking room windows are provided and a separate locking room door below the stairs. The black railings across the sliding casements enable the signalman to lean out when exchanging single line tokens by hand. The nameplate is standard GWR, in cast iron. *Ian Allan Library*

Left:
The simple peak-roof design was executed entirely in timber under a slate roof at Bruern Crossing on the Oxford–Worcester line, seen here in its final days when lifting barriers were being installed. Note the five-paned operating-floor windows which are a well-known hallmark of GWR 'boxes; it also had internal stairs. *Author*

Below:
This dilapidated GWR signalbox shows the main features of the later hipped-roof standard design, although the brick courses at the front are unusual on a 'box which is otherwise of all-timber construction. The five-paned windows feature along with standard pointed roof vents and 'H'-shaped stovepipe chimney. Outside doors lead to an exposed landing. *Real Photographs*

Left:
There were dozens of GWR signalboxes similar to this brick-built example at Bedwyn seen in 1978 just before it was taken out of use. Following the same hipped-roof outline as the wooden version, it usually employed red bricks enlivened with engineers' blues on the corners and around the locking room windows. This example had internal stairs, but many had the traditional wooden external steps. *Author*

Left:
The standard style of Highland Railway signalbox was very distinctive with large windows, a pitched roof and external landing with a small porch. Another unusual feature of the design, seen here at Helmsdale in March 1978, is the vertical board and batten construction. This must have looked fine in Scottish Region light blue and white. *Ray Ruffell*

Right:
Few railways had signalboxes which were more standardised than the Midland. All were built of timber and distinctive features included the pointed finials and angle-topped upper window panes. The 'boxes were of sectional construction, larger examples being produced by adding extra sections. Langham Junction, near Oakham, with its narrow front landing and side windows to the locking room is a typical small example. Oakham 'box is the subject of Dapol 4mm-scale plastic kit. *Author*

Left:
This May 1963 view of Hay station signalbox shows one of the smaller Midland standard 'boxes mounted on a station platform. The metal-step unit was a common feature, as replacement for rotted wooden stairs, but on this 'box it is parallel to the side wall. *Author's collection*

Right:
Almost identical to the signalbox at Hay is this example at Ais Gill on the Midland-built Settle & Carlisle line. In this instance the steps are parallel with the front wall, and the landing extends round three sides of the structure. In 4mm scale a plastic kit for a No 2B Midland 'box, made up of two 10ft sections, is available in the Digby Models 'Melton Line' range. *BR*

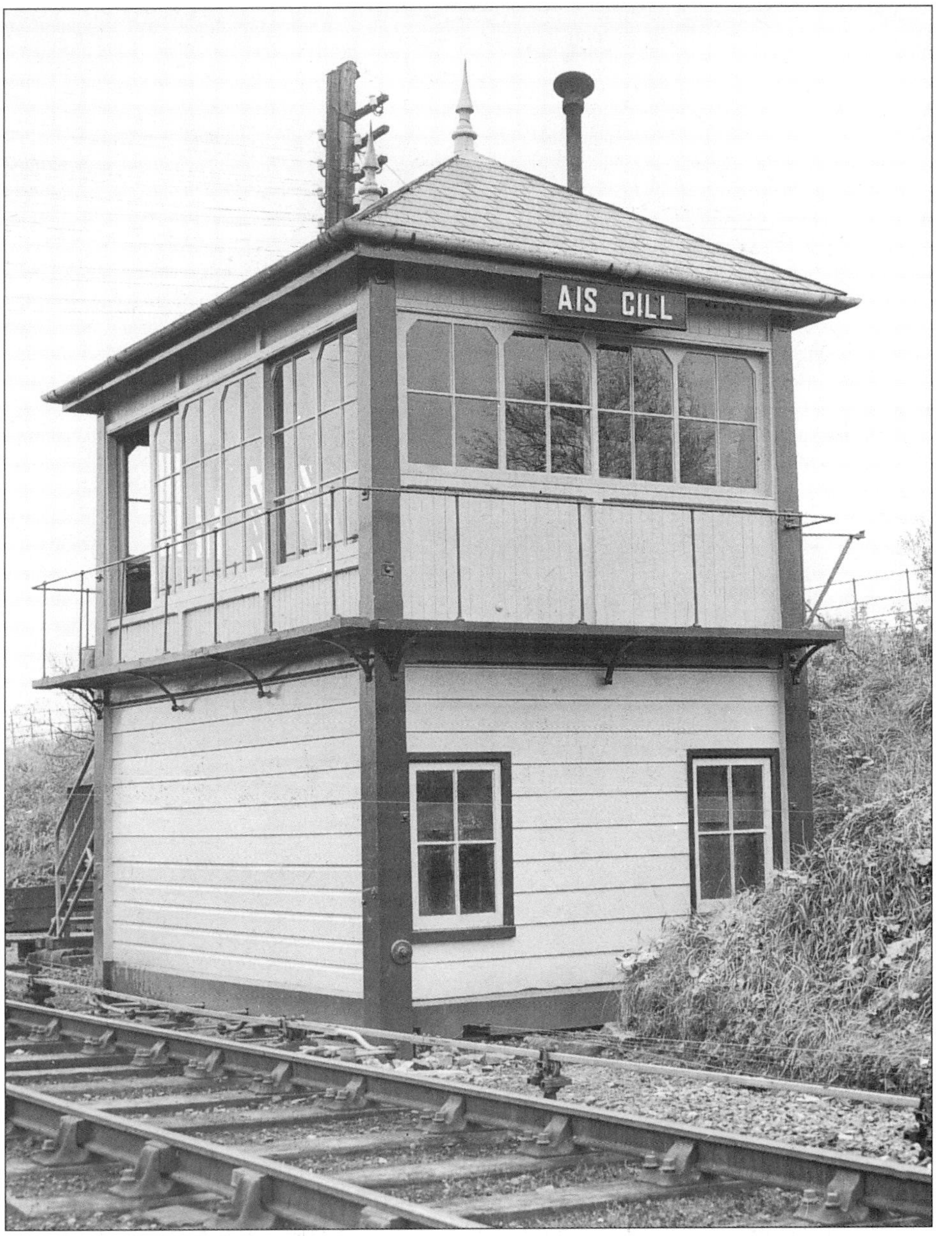

Below:
An interesting rear view of the Great Northern Railway signalbox at Deeping St James, near Stamford. In this area many GNR 'boxes were built of yellow bricks with wooden gable ends and elaborate valancing as seen here. *P. H. Wells*

Left:
Still in existence complete with its lever frame is the 'box at Cowbit (pronounced 'Cubbitt') on the Great Northern & Great Eastern Joint line north of Peterborough. This red-brick box under a slate roof exhibits rather more GN-style features, including the timber gable ends. *Author*

Right:
Now we come to more modern manual signalboxes, with this handsome brick and concrete structure, now out of use, at Spean Bridge on the West Highland line, photographed in 1990. Points to note are the angled front corners, metal window frames, integral brick and concrete stairs and the concrete 'visor' over the main windows. *Author*

Left:
This modern signalbox at Connington North reveals an interesting story because it is seen just after removal to a new location, 75yd from where it was built. The date is 11 May 1954 and the modern brick-built structure is still wearing the substantial braces which have been used to tie it together during the move. An interesting feature of the design is the glazed and illuminated name panel on the roof. *BR*

Left:
One of the elegant brick and concrete Southern Railway signalboxes of the 1930s is seen in March 1970. Though most of these distinctive structures have given way to MAS resignalling, one or two survive — notably that at Templecombe, seen here, which now serves as station facilities at this reopened station. The oval operating floor area was carried on a larger rectangular locking room, and the large nameboard is missing from the front of the structure. *G. R. Hounsell*

Right:
The brick and concrete wartime 'austerity' signalbox at Wellingborough Junction on the Midland main line, seen at the end of its days in 1985. Note the use of concrete for the banisters to the landing on the left-hand end. *David Ingham*

Left:
In the 1960s BR Western Region erected some handsome sectional timber signalboxes like this example at Windsor & Eton Central station. It was built at Reading Signal Works and installed at Windsor in 1963, lasting only until 1968 when the branch was reduced to a long siding. It was then dismantled and re-erected at Viaduct Junction near Kensington Olympia. A slightly larger version of this design was used at Port Talbot Middle. *J. Scrace*

Left:
Another WR structure, but this time in brick and timber, was employed at Machynlleth, as seen here on 31 May 1975. Note that the GWR style of cast plate survives, albeit without the words 'Signal box'. The visor over the windows was a feature of most modern manual signalboxes, being designed to keep the sun off the large expanses of glass. *J. Scrace*

Right:
The modern London Midland Region brick and timber signalbox at Grange-over-Sands seen in May 1979. Note that the metal staircase is similar to those fitted as replacements to certain Midland Railway signalboxes. *J. Scrace*

Left:
The very striking new signalbox at Portishead, Western Region, photographed on 30 December 1953. The brick and timber structure with overhanging roof on the front and sides, and with windows raked outwards at the top, must have seemed extremely modern in its day, despite housing equipment of antiquated design. *BR*

SIGNALBOXES (Power)

MOST power signalboxes of recent years, erected as part of MAS resignalling, have been very large structures at extensive railway locations which are outside the scope of most models. Those selected for illustration have been chosen because they are either quite small or could be reduced to suit modellers' needs. Not all power signalboxes are, of course, modern. Some dated from the pre-Nationalisation railway companies but, by the nature of electrical control systems in those days, they were very large structures indeed.

Above:
Surely the most striking of modern signalboxes was the power 'box at Potters Bar, completed along with the station reconstruction and quadrupling of tracks in November 1955. This light and airy control room atop a plain brick relay room symbolised railway modernisation and was chosen as the prototype for a Merit plastic kit in 4mm scale, now available from Peco. *BR*

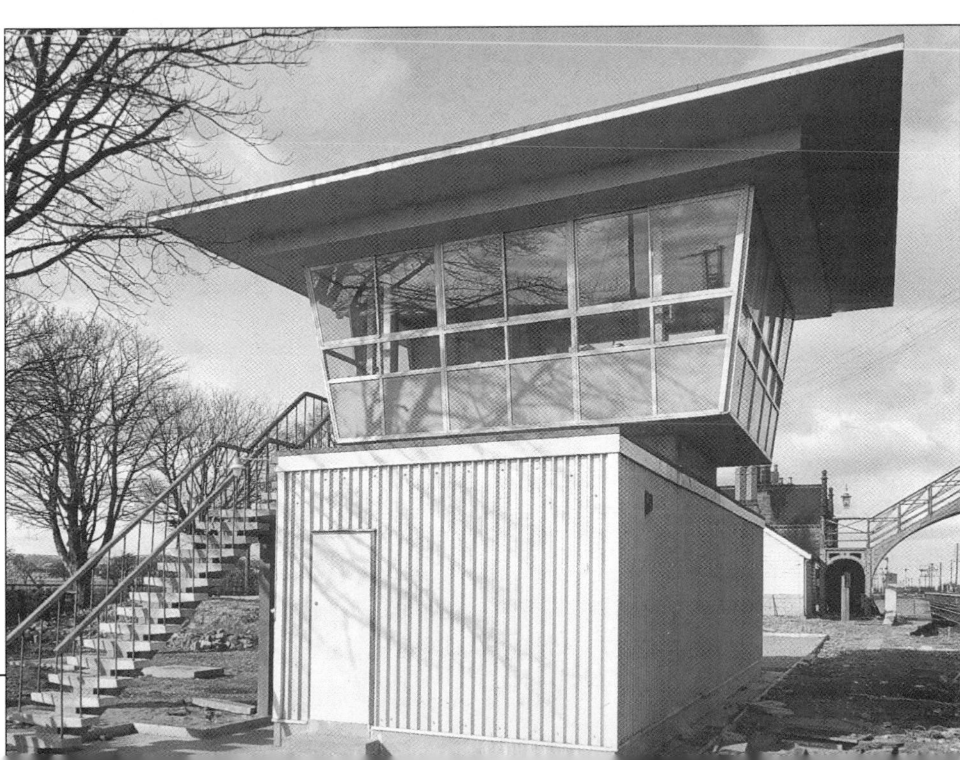

Right:
Taking the Potters Bar style a stage further was the North Eastern Region's Belford of 1962. This 'box with its broad roof shading all-round glass has its relay room clad in corrugated sheeting. *BR*

Top:
The Western Region style of 1962 is seen at East Usk, where the vertical-boarded operating room reflects the style of the small manual 'boxes being built at the same time. The difference is the substantial brick-built relay room on which it stands, presenting a modern but rather austere aspect. *BR*

Above:
Probably too big for the average layout but presenting the Western Region's 'new look' of modernisation was the 1962 signalbox at Old Oak Common with a modernistic control room with angled glass on top of a blue-brick relay room and attached imitation stone messrooms. *BR*

SIGNALS (Colour Light)

SIGNALLING is a specialist section of railway interest and a number of books dealing with its intricacies are available, such as *BR Signalling Handbook* by Stanley Hall, published by Ian Allan. Such books give information on the layout, siting and general arrangement of correct signalling practice. It is too lengthy a subject to cover in detail here. However, this section does include some illustrations of typical signals to aid the modeller. The introduction of colour light signalling enabled complex mechanical installations to be replaced by wiring and low-maintenance electrical equipment. Maintenance costs were reduced and train speeds could be increased once the labour-intensive mechanical signalbox gave way to miniature levers operating electrical switches and relays.

Left:
Early colour light signals, such as this 1930s example on the LNER, were often of the 'searchlight' type in which coloured lenses changed the signal aspect through a single hooded 'searchlight'. The row of five white lights is known as a 'feather' and indicates that the route is set for the train to diverge to the left at the next junction. *BR*

Right:
These variants of the 'searchlight' signal are also seen on the LNER York–Darlington resignalling of the 1930s. On such main line routes the advance of technology would have seen such signals replaced in the BR era, and again with electrification. *BR*

Left:
A 'searchlight' signal of the BR era at Thorpe-le-Soken in February 1959. This signal was erected as part of the Colchester–Clacton electrification. It has a left-hand 'feather' for the crossover beyond it. The white diamond plate indicates that the signal is covered by a track circuit, so a waiting train driver does not have to telephone the signalman to remind him of the train's presence, under Rule 55. *BR*

Below:
The most recent BR signal installations have been MAS (multiple aspect signalling) schemes where whole areas have been converted to signalling with three- (or more recently) four-aspect colour lights controlled from one signalling centre. These three-aspect (red, amber, green) signals were part of the Newport scheme, photographed when new in May 1961. In 4mm:1ft scale, operating colour light signals are included in the Eckon range. *BR*

A tremendous mixture of signals is seen during the changeover to MAS at Bristol Temple Meads in 1970. In the foreground new MAS colour lights with route indicators above are covered with 'X' plates to indicate that they are not in use. Beyond them stand the round-topped 1934 colour lights which they are to replace. In the left background is a GWR lower quadrant semaphore. *BR*

Above:
A modern MAS ground signal controlling access from a siding on to the main line. The bottom left indication is red, indicating 'stop', as the right-hand white light shows that the catch points are set to protect the main line. With the road set for the main line the white light would be extinguished and the top (green) aspect would be illuminated. A lineside telephone allows the train crew to communicate with the signalbox when they are ready to leave.
Author's Collection

SIGNALS (Semaphore)

SEMAPHORE signalling practice is too large a topic to deal with in detail here, but fortunately there are substantial volumes available on the signalling of the 'Big Four' companies. The styles of semaphore signal fit three broad categories: lower quadrant, in which the arm drops from the horizontal stop position to 'clear', upper quadrant, in which the arm rises from horizontal to 'clear', and somersault in which the arm pivots away from the post to near vertical on the 'clear' indication. A few examples are illustrated in order to give a general guide.

Above:
Great Western Railway lower quadrant signals were built of timber until the late 1920s, but many timber examples survived right through the BR steam era to be replaced eventually by colour lights. Framing a 'Grange' 4-6-0 at Grafton East Junction near Savernake in 1951 is a splendid bracket with a wooden post, wooden 'doll' (the short supplementary post) and wooden arms. The lamps and a GWR finial can also be seen. The post is also serving as a telegraph pole. The distinctive GWR finials had the ball part painted red except on posts having only 'distant' arms, when the ball was painted yellow. *D. E. H. Box*

Below:
Controlling the exit from the Wycombe branch bay at Maidenhead was this GWR tubular-post signal. The GWR used tubular steel posts from about the 1920s onwards. This one has main and shunt home arms of flat steel plate, a 'theatre'-type route indicator below, and carries a track circuit diamond. The route indicator would display two letters indicating 'main' or 'branch' routes obviating the need for a bracket signal. *Author's collection*

Above:
A standard lattice post upper quadrant with steel arm on the West Highland Extension at Arisaig in 1972. *Andrew Muckley*

Left:
Reading General station in the 1950s. The wooden-post bracket signal has had replacement metal arms fitted. These arms had the distinctive fluted edges, unlike the metal arms fitted to the later tubular posts which were flat. Note the track circuit diamond plates identical to those later fitted to colour light signals. *Author's collection*

Right:
The rear view of the down home signal at Colnbrook station in about 1965. The signal is a standard GWR tubular-post structure, but the arm is mounted lower down the post than usual so that it can be seen below the station canopy. The steel ladder and hoop enabled the regular servicing of the oil lamp. *Ian Allan Library*

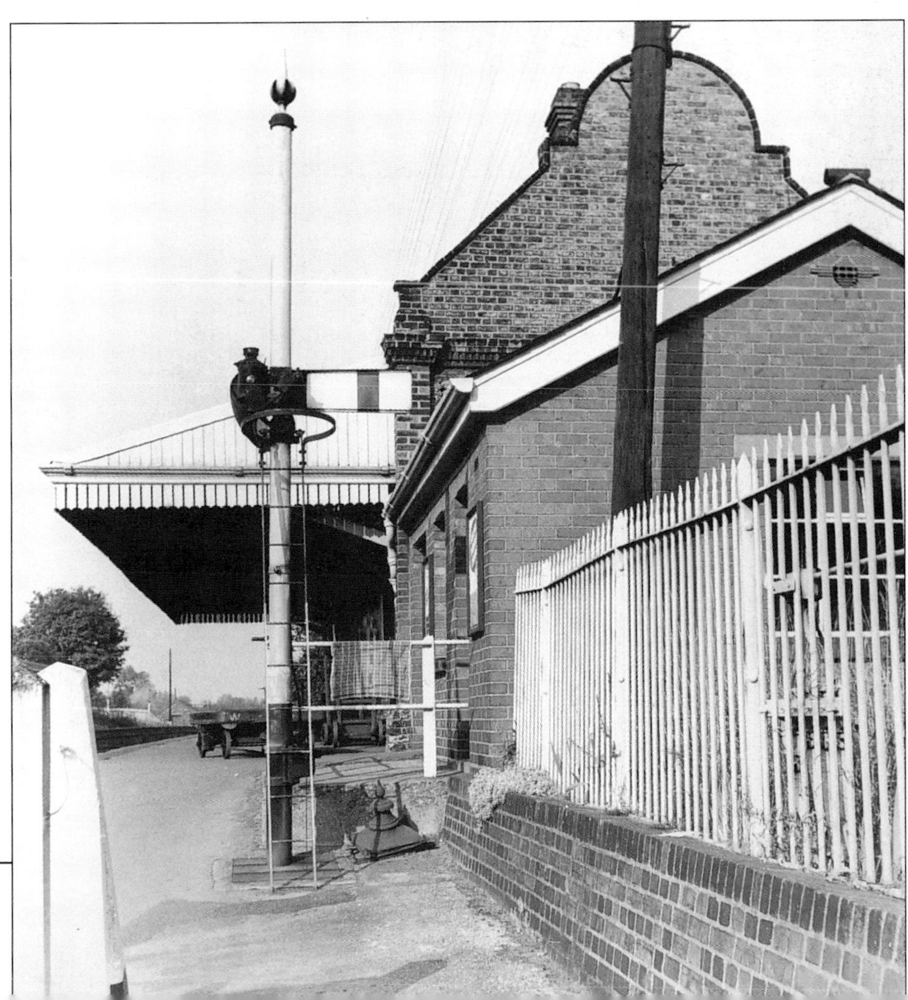

Left:
A typical GWR tubular-post bracket signal is seen at Bourne End in the mid-1960s with the addition of a shunt 'doll' in the centre. This junction arrangement has a tall 'doll' for the main line ahead to Maidenhead (from the down platform where Marlow–Maidenhead trains reversed) and a shorter doll to control the divergence to the right on to the Marlow branch. The line on the extreme right terminated in a bay platform. *Ian Allan Library*

Below left:
Very different from the GWR is the style of lower quadrant seen at Norwich City station in BR days. This cast concrete bracket signal dates from the days of the Midland & Great Northern Joint Railway and has long slender wooden arms. Note the two substantial concrete posts to which the signal is anchored with guy wires. *Real Photographs*

Right:
An LSWR lattice post is seen fitted with an upper quadrant arm at Medstead & Four Marks station in the 1960s. Although the Southern Railway standardised on upper quadrant signals, some LSWR lower quadrants survived into BR days. *Ian Allan Library*

Below right:
A bracket junction signal with LMS steel arms on a timber post and steel bracket assembly at Harecastle Tunnel in the 1950s. *BR*

Above:
An incredibly spidery lattice-post lower quadrant signal of London & South Western origin controls the approach to Woody Bay station on the narrow gauge Lynton & Barnstaple Railway. Even the finial is a lattice construction. The signal was particularly high in order to bring the arm well clear of the adjacent bridge so that it could be clearly seen from approaching trains. *F. E. Box/Ian Allan Library*

Below:
Now we come to a variety of different types of BR upper quadrant semaphores located on the former Eastern and Midland Regions of BR. First, the up starter at Millbrook on the Bedford–Bletchley line employs a simple tubular steel post, 'waisted' just over half-way up, and with a neat round cap. The arm is steel plate and there is a fabricated steel ladder and hoop. *Author*

Above right:
A standard BR-bracket installation re-erected on the Nene Valley Railway at Peterborough shows the same post style and main arm. A stout bracket supports the subsidiary tubular 'doll' with its smaller arm. A white sighting board is fitted and both arms carry the 'X' to indicate that the signal is not in use. *Author*

Right:
A rear view of a standard BR stop signal which shows clearly how the sighting board is placed behind the arm, which is 'off' for an approaching Class 158 at Whittlesey in 1994. *Author*

Left:
The BR standard starting signal at County School station has the 'waist' lower down the post. The counterweight is clearly seen in this 1994 view of a signal acquired from BR and repositioned on a private railway. *Author*

Above:
The use of a bracket post for sighting purposes is demonstrated by the starter at Oulton Broad North where a very large sighting board is placed behind the arm to eliminate confusing backgrounds. A track-circuited signal with low 'waist' to the post and a deep brace to the bracket platform. October 1994. *Author*

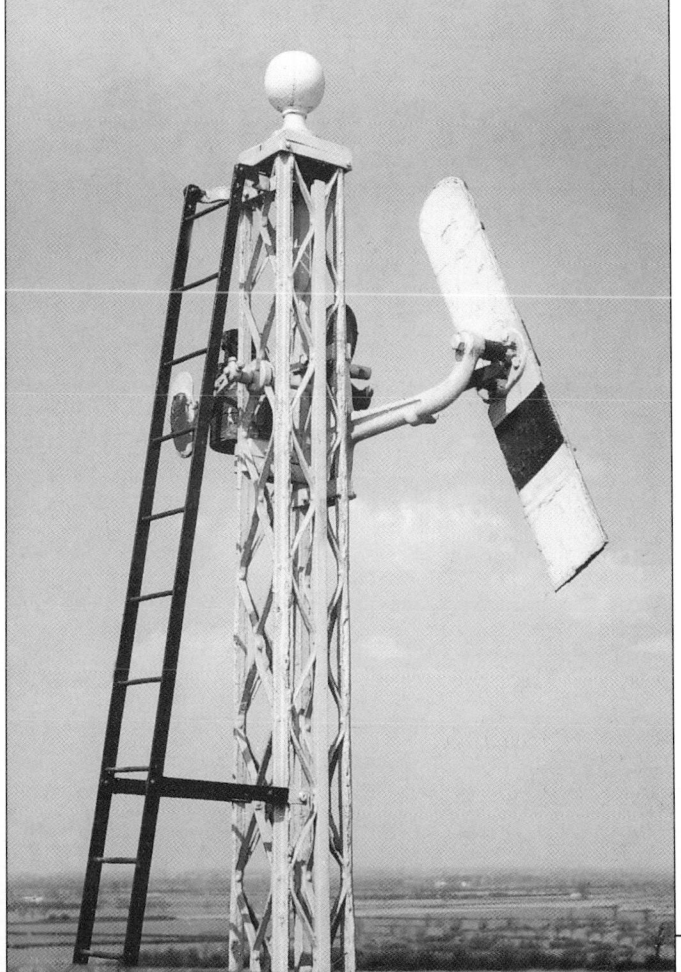

Left:
Somersault signals generally date from pre-1923 and a few still survive on BR. The up home at Leadenham, Great Northern Railway, with wooden arm and lattice post, is seen in close-up on 8 April 1953. The GNR was a big user of somersault signals. *R. O. Tuck*

Right:
A somersault distant signal with typical Midland & Great Northern Railway concrete post seen in February 1959. On this example the spectacle glass is positioned much lower down the posts than the arm. *Real Photographs (R8911)*

Below:
A concrete post GNR somersault signal surviving in 1979. It protected the crossing at Roxton Sidings on the Doncaster–Grimsby line, alongside a very fine board and batten signalbox. *Les Nixon*

SIGNS & NOTICES (Lineside)

LINESIDE signs fall into two distinct categories: those for the attention of railway staff (which generally had to be observed from a moving train) and those intended for the information or warning of the public. Whilst the former had to be designed for the clearest possible visibility, those for the public generally related to public crossings or matters of trespass and the public were expected to stop and read them.

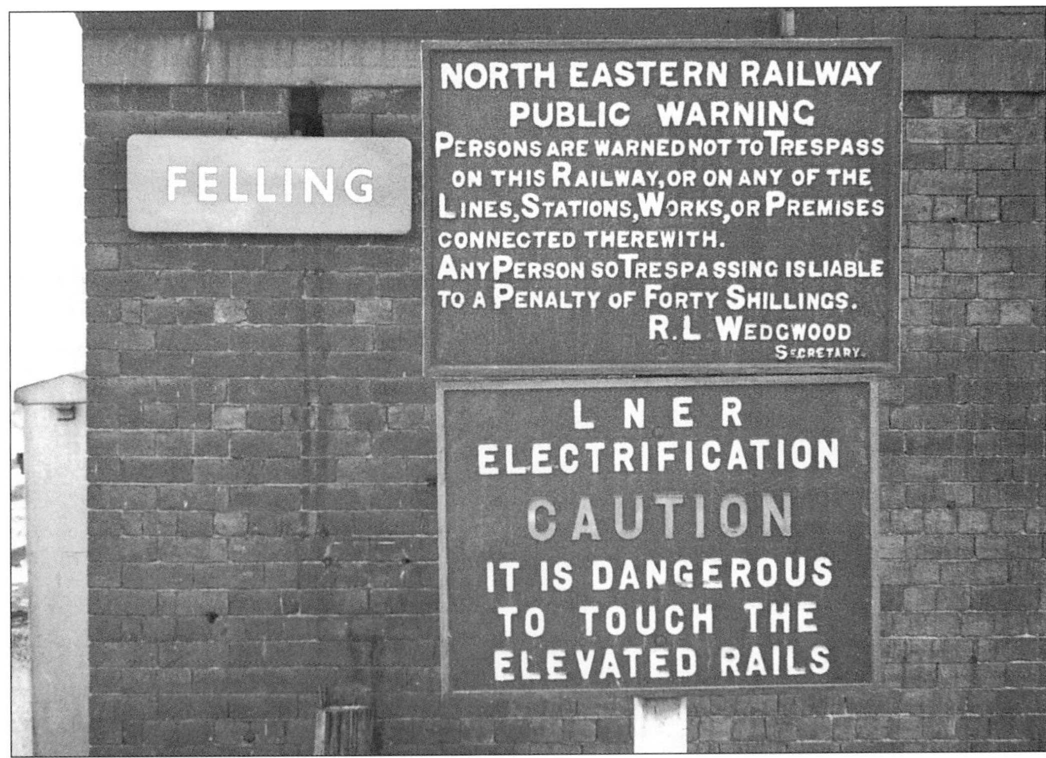

Right:
Public warning notices were designed for durability and the use of cast-iron plates with raised lettering picked out in white paint was common practice. This view shows a pre-1923 North Eastern Railway cast trespass notice above a later LNER example warning of live rails on the Newcastle electrification — seen in 1964. *I. S. Carr*

Right:
This North British Railway cast trespass notice is one which quotes the relevant parliamentary act and the standard penalty. Such notices lasted well into the 1960s despite changes in legislation and currency, but today it is rare to find one still in place. *A. McLean*

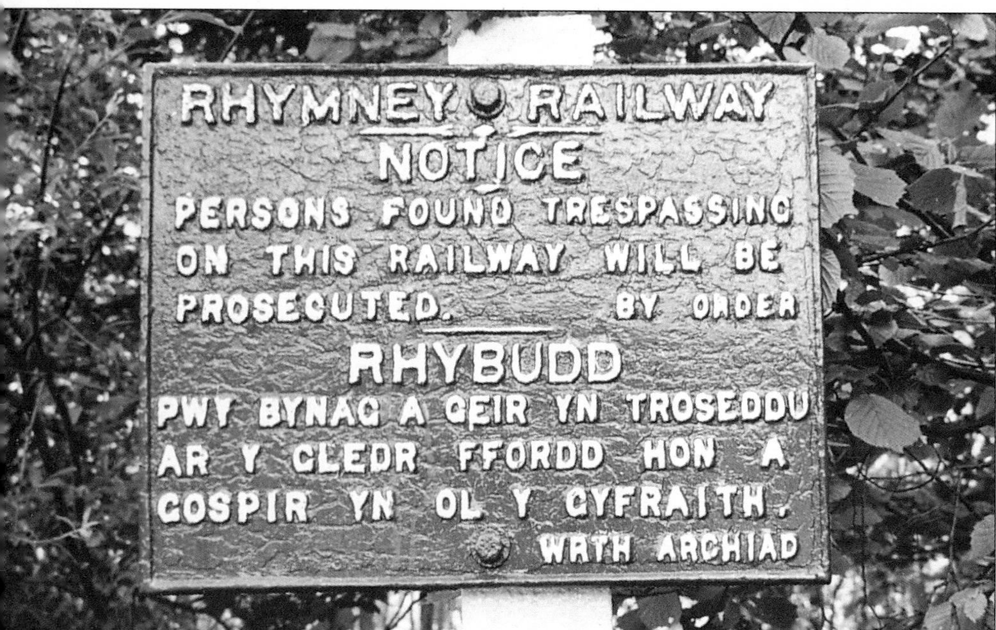

Left:
In Wales, many cast notices were bilingual. This pre-1923 Rhymney Railway trespass notice was at Cefn-On halt and survived in the 1960s. *Ian Allan Library*

Right:
Some cast-iron plates could be very large. The Great Western used a large plate to warn passengers not to cross the line — the bilingual version seen here was even larger. *E. K. Stretch*

Left:
This SECR cast trespass notice was still in place on the Reading–Tonbridge line in 1977 and had been simply amended with white paint to increase the penalty to £25. *Ray Ruffell*

Left:
Joint lines produced some rare combinations of title on cast notices. The Midland and the GWR came together at Berkeley, where this unusual trespass notice still survived in 1963. The 'Beware of Trains' appears to be an MR plate and both are affixed to a stout timber post by square-headed bolts. *E. Wilmshurst*

Below:
Despite its 'Caution' heading, this is a trespass notice of the London & North Western Railway, photographed as the Stamford–Seaton push-pull passed on 27 September 1965. *P. H. Wells*

Left:
The GWR used timber boards with cast-iron letters for most of its larger notices. These 'Stop' boards were placed at the top of inclines as an instruction to train crews. Usually black and white in GWR days and brown and cream in the days of BR Western Region, this example was photographed in the 1970s when painted red with white letters. It was at Lightmoor Junction. *Author*

Below left:
Concrete posts were commonplace on the Midland & Great Northern Joint Line. This cast trespass notice was as brief as it could possibly be. Photographed at Bourne in June 1968. *P. H. Wells*

Below:
Like 'Raising the Flag at Iwo Jima', the permanent way crew erects the first 100mph speed limit sign on the East Coast main line, between Stoke summit and Lolham in June 1964. These cut-out metal speed signs, of welded construction, are still used to indicate the maximum line speed and can vary from 5 to 125mph. The post is black and the figures are painted yellow. *BR*

Right:
Railway quarter-mile posts varied from one company to another, some using either dots or bars to indicate the quarters. This double arrangement with two faces at right angles, placed at an angle to the track, was the norm. Milepost $52^{3}/_{4}$ was photographed between Ashford and Pluckley, Kent, in 1951. *R. E. Vincent*

Below:
Lineside posters which faced the railway were not common outside urban areas. However, the brewer Strong & Co of Romsey, Hampshire, certainly placed its mark on the railways of that county with hoardings such as this, featuring a stylized Bulleid 'Pacific'. *Ian Allan Library*

SIGNS & NOTICES (Station)

THE signs and notices employed on stations were, and are, primarily for the information of the public. At all stations, no matter how large or small, it was necessary to indicate the name of the station and the location which it served. This was done with large name signs on posts near the platform ends at the 'approach' end of each platform and often at the 'departure' end as well. On most stations these were supplemented by names applied to the lamp posts or to the glass fronts of gas lamps. The larger boards are often referred to as 'running in boards'. Other station signs might indicate directions to different platforms or denote offices such as the ticket office, left luggage office, parcels or waiting rooms. Areas reserved for use by staff only were simply marked 'Private'.

Though standardised with the advent of corporate image during the late 1960s, a fascinating variety survived until quite recently, and with sectorisation in the 1980s further variety became evident. In his range of 4mm:1ft station fittings Chris Leigh includes running in boards for each of the 'Big Four' companies, plus BR and Network SouthEast.

Above:
My selection of running in boards starts with the distinctive style of the Mid-Suffolk Light Railway, which employed a wooden board with fluted border, mounted on rail posts. The attractive 'rustic' lettering was cast iron. This was a 1951 view. *H. C. Casserley*

Below:
This is a Great Western Railway station nameboard mounted on the company's usual round cast-iron posts. The board was timber with a plain border, rather wider than usual. The sanserif cast-iron letters were 12in but smaller alphabets were available — down to 1in for certain notices. This board measured 8ft by 2ft 6in but boards were constructed to any size to suit the name. In 4mm:1ft scale, posts are produced by Dart Castings and complete boards are available from Chris Leigh, Mikes Models and Coopercraft. *Ian Allan Library*

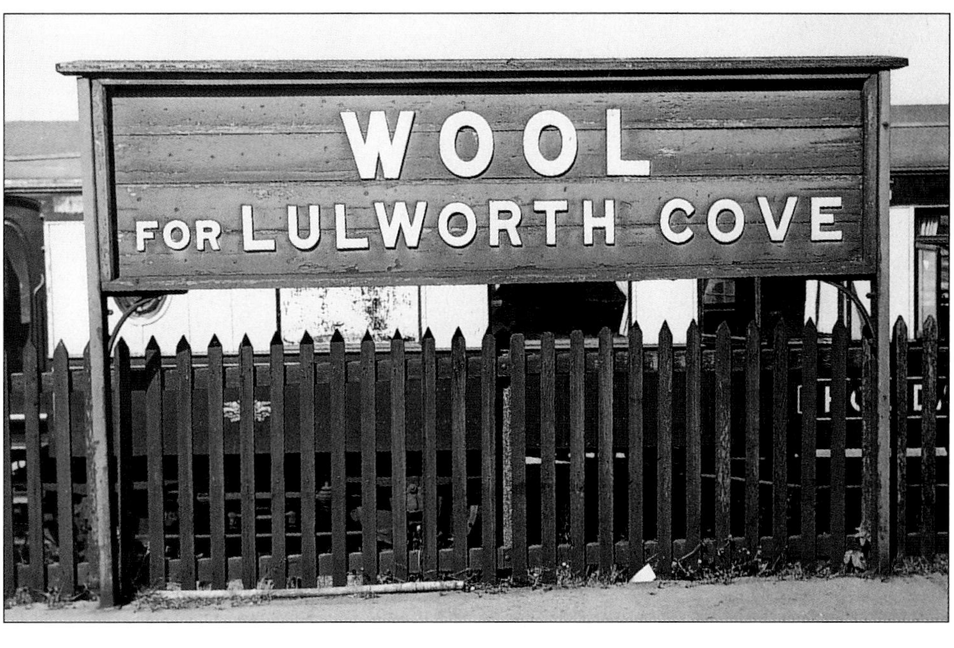

Right:
Another example of a wooden board with cast-iron letters is this London & South Western Railway example in SR condition — painted green with white letters. The rail posts are bolted to the ends of the board and a wooden capping piece is fitted. A 1966 view. The Chris Leigh range of 4mm:1ft accessories includes a narrower version of this style. *John Scrace*

Left:
Again, separate letters are mounted on a large board at this Waverley Route station, and smaller letters are used to give the supplementary information. The layout of the station name suggests that this was the maximum size of board available. *Ian Allan Library*

Right:
Simple, elegant posts and architrave result in a very attractive board of London & North Western Railway origin, seen in 1926. S. *Osbornellan Allan Library*

Left:
Lots of these attractive Highland Railway running in boards survived into the BR era, this example lasting to be photographed in 1971. Square timber posts are topped by signal-type ball-and-spike finials. Separate cast-iron letters are used, though on some boards the Scottish Region replaced these with its own blue and white enamel plates. A cast metal version of this board is available in 4mm:1ft scale in the Chris Leigh range. *Andrew Muckley*

Below:
The stylish modern 1935 station at Elm Park includes running in boards of standard LMS style with a seat built around the base. On the usual pattern of these boards the flat plate was replaced with a raised 'bulls-eye' border and separate cast letters. *LMS/Ian Allan Library*

Right:
Turning to signs other than running in boards, the LNWR station at Heaton Chapel shows an array of typical examples suspended from the canopy. Separate cast letters are used and the pointing finger is also a standard casting — as typically Victorian as the 'arrow' is modern. *Ian Allan Library*

Below right:
A mind-blowing array of signs, posters and advertisements greeted the passenger at this platform entrance on Liverpool Central station, probably in the 1930s, but the view is credited to the British Transport Commission and could have been taken after Nationalisation to show the station before re-signing. *BR*

LADIES
FIRST CLASS
WAITING ROOM
GENTLEMEN'S
FIRST CLASS
WAITING ROOM
GENERAL
WAITING ROOM
WAY OUT
HEATON CHAPEL

QUICKEST ROUTE BETWEEN
LIVERPOOL — BIRKENHEAD — WIRRAL PENINSULA
AND THE
GREAT WESTERN AND LONDON MIDLAND & SCOTTISH
RAILWAY SYSTEMS
THROUGH BOOKINGS
TO
THE WIRRAL PENINSULA
NORTH AND SOUTH WALES
MIDLANDS
SOUTH AND WEST
OF ENGLAND
MERSEY
RAILWAY
LEYLAND
CAMP COFFEE
LIFEBUOY SOAP
VIROL
FINNIGANS
MERSEY RAILWAY
THROUGH CONNECTIONS
CHEAP DAY TICKETS
CHEAP TICKETS
HIGSONS
TROJAN
TO GENTLEMEN'S HAIRDRESSING
& TOILET SALOON
LNER
MERSEY RAILWAY
ELECTRIC TRAINS EVERY FEW MINUTES
WHITBREAD'S
LONDON STOUT
INDIA PALE ALE

Left:
Some of the elaborate features of the pre-Grouping era survived right into BR days. This etched-glass window of the refreshment room at Dereham station incorporated the arms of the Great Eastern Railway. *W. S. Garth*

Right:
At some unstaffed halts, notably on the GWR, tickets were sold at nearby locations. At Farrington Gurney, the local public house sold rail tickets; at Dilton Marsh, a nearby resident sold them from a private house; and at Appleford halt near Didcot, they were sold from the village Post Office. This sign, made up from cast-iron letters on a timber board would have carried either 'Great Western Railway' or 'GWR' on the blank top line. BR, Western Region, either removed the letters or painted out the 'Great' or 'G' when necessary.
R. E. Vincent

Below:
Pre-Grouping designations still lingered on these Carlisle station blackboards in June 1937. Platform details of departing trains were chalked up for the information of passengers.
H. C. Casserley

Above:
Before its adoption of cast-iron letters as standard, the GWR used enamelled plates — usually blue lettering on white for all signs except running in boards where the colours were reversed. This weather-worn example adorned the gate of the station house at Colnbrook and lasted into the 1970s.
Author

Top:
From very soon after Nationalisation, British Railways began its programme of standardised signing, using enamelled metal plates in the six chosen regional colours. Here, a two-part enamelled plate in Eastern Region dark blue with white letters, has been applied to a timber running in board of earlier origin and still stands in 1974. The Gill Sans typeface was adopted as standard for all BR signs. *R. I. Wallace*

Above:
A distinctive feature of the 1950s BR signs was the totem or 'double-sausage' which became the BR logo and was used in a variety of roles from headed notepaper to station signs. On stations, the totem was used adjacent to lamps and in addition to the running in boards. Hexham featured an early example of the North Eastern Region white on orange scheme, with the letters outlined in black. Nowadays it would be a very desirable piece of railwayana. *Ian Allan Library*

Top:
Darlington Bank Top, also in NER orange and white, is a version without the black outlining but also shows how the supplementary parts of the name were incorporated in the bottom segment of the sign. A 1953 view. *R. E. Vincent*

Above:
A climbing rose engulfing the lamp post does not obscure the simple design and easy legibility of the BR standard signs. Dersingham, on the Hunstanton branch, was photographed in 1968, by which time the totem had already been displaced by BR's new corporate image. *G. R. Mortimer*

Left:
At Cowden on the Southern Region a green and white totem has replaced the etched-glass name in this handsome gas lantern. *H. M. Wright*

Above:
Only the Western Region did not use white for the lettering on its totems, preferring to continue the tradition of chocolate brown and cream, though oddly enough, the GWR had not used these colours for its station signs, which were usually black and white. In the mid-1960s one or two Thames Valley area stations received black and white totems. Kemble was signed throughout in chocolate and cream BR enamel, even featuring unique direction signs 'Tetbury Train' and 'Cirencester Train' pointing to its two branch platforms. *Author*

Right:
A fascinating close-up taken at Surbiton in 1946 shows the new-style Southern Railway enamel signing on which BR must have based its style — for the BR platform signs were virtually identical to this example in which enamelled, pressed plates are assembled back-to-back and suspended from the canopy by 'eyes' and chains. *Southern Railway/Ian Allan Library*

Below:
The standard BR running in board of the 1950s featured pressed metal plates fixed back-to-back and lettered both sides where necessary. The plates were enamelled and the lettering was the Gill Sans standard. Tubular metal posts were used, there being a spacer piece between the post and board. This example has built-in illumination, but not all of them did. A similar board is included in Chris Leigh's 4mm:1ft range of cast accessories. In this installation the board is 'offset' — placed at an angle to the running lines rather than parallel to them. *BR*

Left:
A double-line version of the BR standard running in board, photographed when new in December 1956. This example also incorporates lights. Though the Southern Region painted the tubular posts green, most other Regions painted them black, as seen here on the WR. *BR*

Below:
Plain flat enamelled plates were used where they could be mounted on a solid background. The goods depot at Britain's oldest railway station incorporated such a sign, in LMR maroon with the BR totem. *John Clarke*

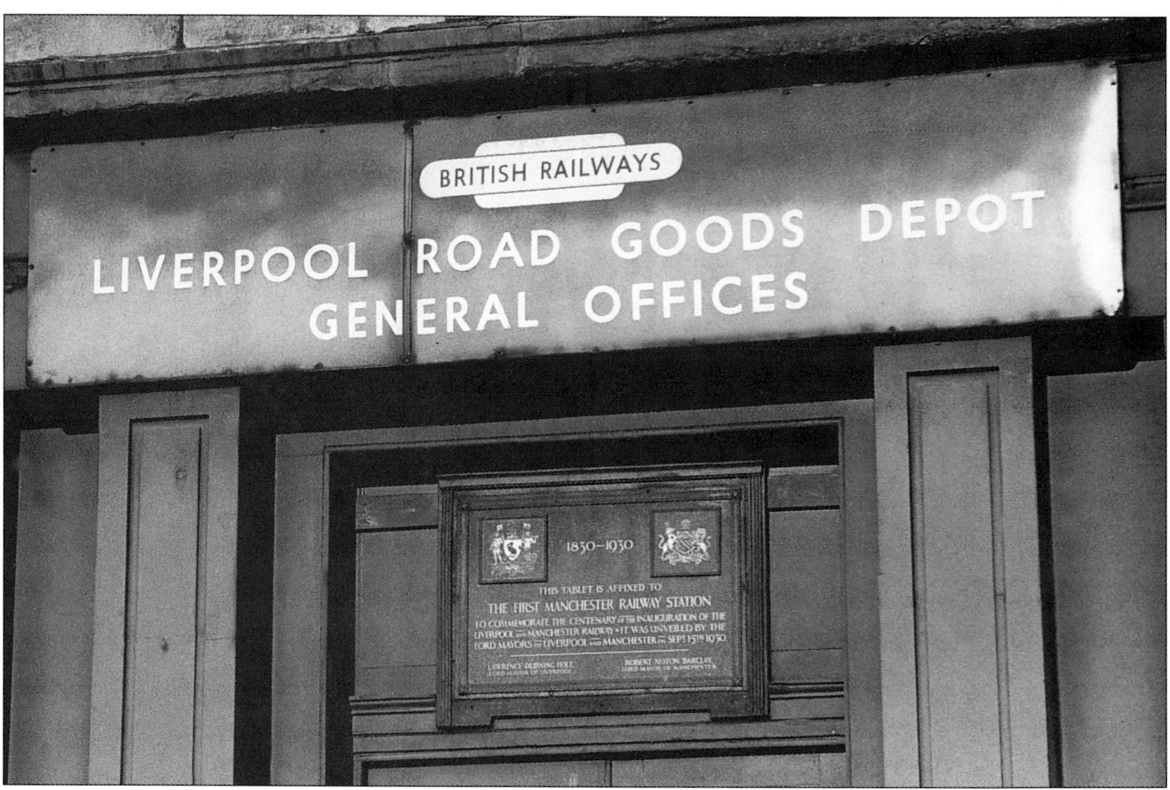

Left:
Miraculously still in place in 1994 was this large four-part dark blue Eastern Region plate on the exterior of a crumbling Lowestoft Central station. *Author*

Above:
At some locations where no major modernisation work was planned, steps were taken to upgrade some of the details. At Clapham Junction in 1967 an illuminated running in board is seen. This had opaque letters on a semi-opaque box structure, inside of which were fluorescent lights. The design was more effective at night than in the daytime when it took on the general aura of its scruffy steam-age surroundings. *A. McIntyre*

Below:
A piece of elegant modernity which pre-dates BR is seen at Finsbury Park in 1944. The modern precast concrete post carries a simple board which uses the Gill Sans typeface — the 'standard' typeface of the transport industry, chosen because of the high legibility of its capital letters. It is shown as 'experimental' in the photograph which is dated 9 August 1944. *LNER/Ian Allan Library*

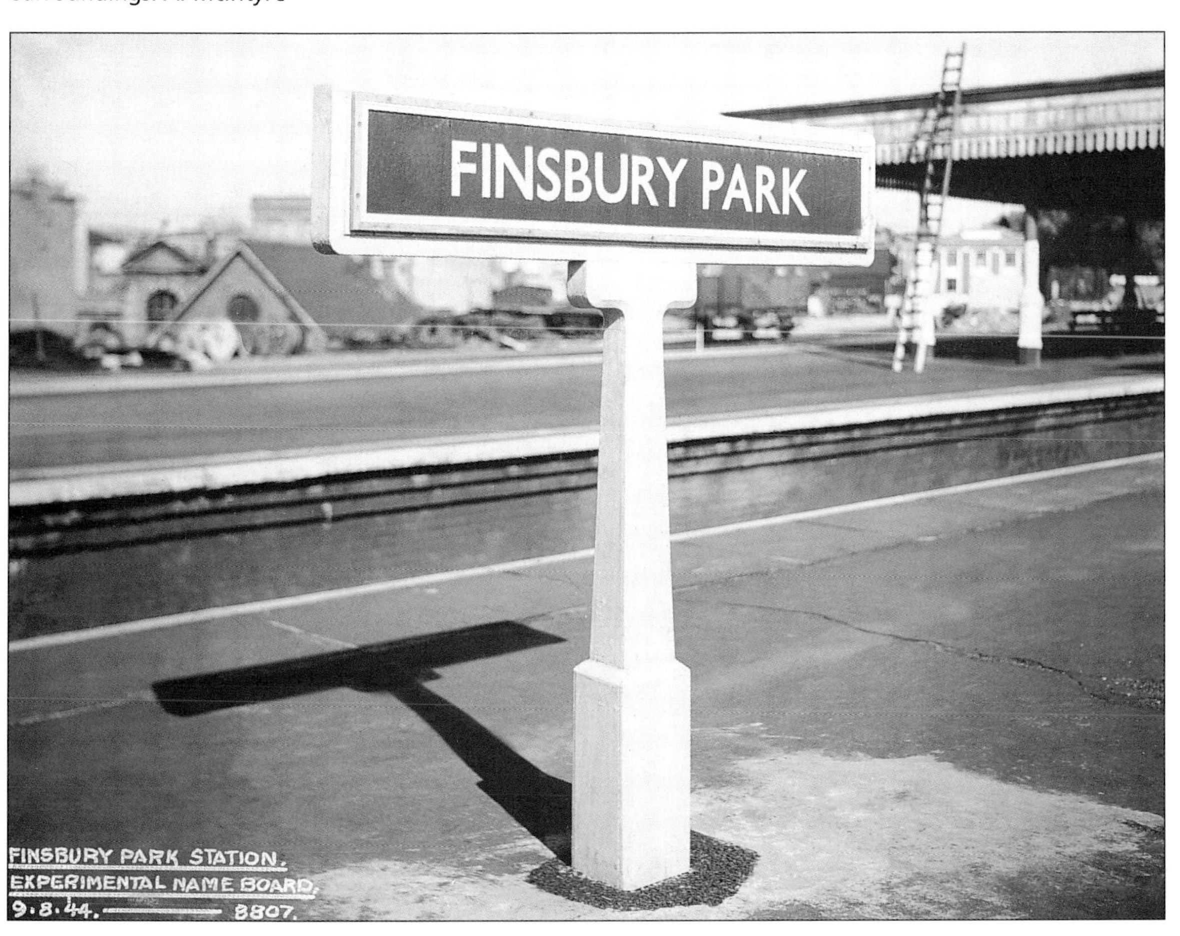

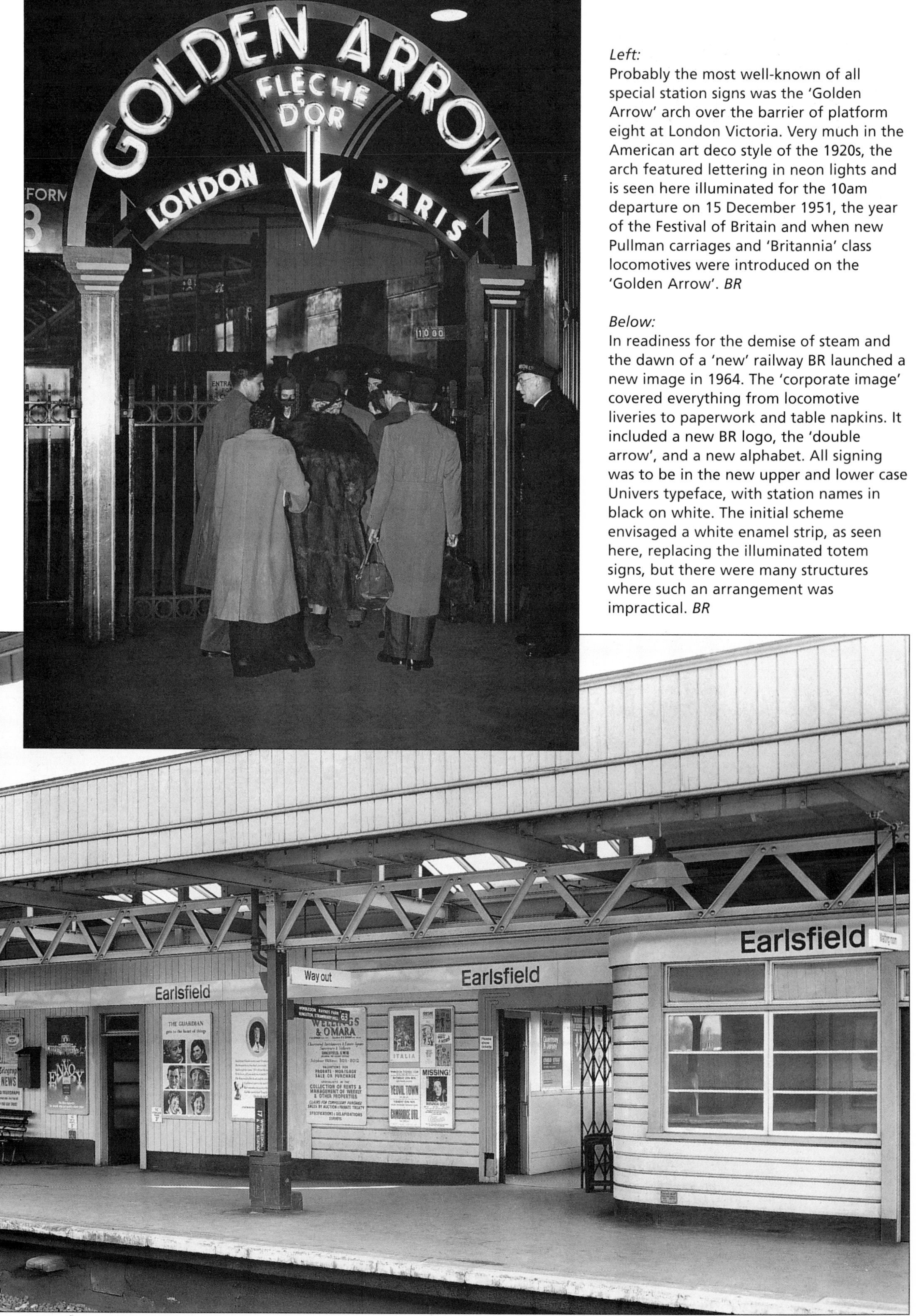

Left:
Probably the most well-known of all special station signs was the 'Golden Arrow' arch over the barrier of platform eight at London Victoria. Very much in the American art deco style of the 1920s, the arch featured lettering in neon lights and is seen here illuminated for the 10am departure on 15 December 1951, the year of the Festival of Britain and when new Pullman carriages and 'Britannia' class locomotives were introduced on the 'Golden Arrow'. *BR*

Below:
In readiness for the demise of steam and the dawn of a 'new' railway BR launched a new image in 1964. The 'corporate image' covered everything from locomotive liveries to paperwork and table napkins. It included a new BR logo, the 'double arrow', and a new alphabet. All signing was to be in the new upper and lower case Univers typeface, with station names in black on white. The initial scheme envisaged a white enamel strip, as seen here, replacing the illuminated totem signs, but there were many structures where such an arrangement was impractical. *BR*

Above:
The 'double arrow' representing up and down tracks was intended to become synonymous with the railway. It was a highly successful feature of the corporate image, despite being derided at the time as 'the arrow of indecision'. This example was outside High Wycombe station, and the standard style was white on a red background. *BR*

Above right:
In this form the sign would appear in white on a rail-blue background. Throughout the early corporate image era, signs continued to be enamelled on metal plates, though signs erected during the 1970s and after often used a printed plastic white which became dirty or broken much more readily. *BR*

Below:
The standard alphabet as it appeared on suspended station signs, in black lettering with rail-blue arrows. All these so-called 'plank' signs were a standard length regardless of the length of wording. Where the words were too long, a second line was added and the depth increased. Corporate image signs are available in various scales in the Tiny Signs range. *BR*

Left:
The application of corporate image at small rural stations included the replacement of running-in boards with these neat but flimsy replacements. Again, the lettering and posts were black with the enamelled metal plate in white. *M. Soden*

Below:
The standard corporate image was adapted only slightly in the 1980s when BR's Provincial Sector became Regional Railways. While Network SouthEast and InterCity went for a whole new image, Regional retained the double arrow and corporate signware at most of its stations, replacing only the platform running in boards and totems with its own variant. This is the road approach and ticket office at Whittlesey in 1994. *Author*

Left:
The Regional Railways totem employs the standard corporate image alphabet with Regional's dark-blue stripe with three white bars below the name. A tubular post supports this totem, but some are fitted to lamp standards. *Author*

Below:
A rear view of the large pattern running in board used by Network SouthEast. Tubular steel posts are inset from the ends of a simple enamelled plate. The front is enamelled in white with the words 'Network SouthEast welcome to...' followed by the place name in the corporate image alphabet. NSE red, blue and grey colours are used. A similar style of NSE board is included in Chris Leigh's 4mm:1ft scale range. *Author*

Left:
An array of modern standard signs and other fittings are seen at the platform end of Crianlarich station in 1991, including the stop boards with their large red circle warning drivers to obtain the single-line token and permission to proceed into the next single-track section. Radio Electronic Token Block (RETB) signalling is employed, the token being 'given' and 'received' by radio link. *Author*

STABLES

RAILWAYS owned thousands of horses in the 19th century, both for shunting work and for local road deliveries. Indeed, not until the mid-1960s was the last railway horse retired. Many station goods yards were provided with stables for the local delivery horses and they varied in size according to the amount of work and the number of horses involved. As the motor lorry and Scammell 'mechanical horses' took over local deliveries, so some stables were converted to garages by installing large doors.

Right:
The GWR stables at Shipton-for-Burford seen derelict in the 1970s. The door was reached by a ramp. The windows had timber frames with cast-iron 'hit-and-miss' ventilators below. Inside, wooden partitions divided the structure into stalls. This building was of red brick under a grey slate roof. A slightly larger building to the same general design was provided at Chipping Norton, but built of alternating courses of red and blue bricks. It was subsequently altered to a motor lorry garage by setting a pair of large wooden doors into one end. *Author*

STATION BUILDINGS

THIS section features main station buildings, that is the structure containing the booking hall and other essential station offices. In some of these structures there was also living accommodation for the stationmaster or a member of staff. The selection — from thousands of possible subjects — concentrates on those structures which are of a modest size and therefore suitable as potential subjects for a typical layout. Large city stations, and indeed many small country branch line stations, have been well covered in specific books, so there is little point in covering them in great detail here. The aim of this section, therefore, is to provide a taste of the styles of station architecture to be found on each of the 'Big Four' railway companies, to aid modellers in making an initial choice.

In many instances they will be able to find more detailed published records of the station they have chosen, and research in local libraries and the booklists of specialist railway publishers are recommended.

Owing to the large number of stations featured here, this section is sub-divided into the main BR Regions as far as possible.

LONDON MIDLAND REGION

Below:
Where the Furness Railway line from Carnforth to Barrow-in-Furness reaches the shore of the Kent Estuary and then turns to cross it, stands the little station of Arnside. The small sturdy brick building is seen here in the 1960s, its exposed position necessitating a low and well-built structure. Red brick and a simple gable roof of slate and low chimney stacks, are the salient features. There was a somewhat larger building on the other platform. *Ian Allan Library*

Below:
Cressington station, a former Cheshire Lines Committee structure south of Liverpool centre and close to the Mersey, was photographed in 1979 following a successful refurbishment. Its position in a shallow cutting allows an imposing structure on three floors, which is entered from the street at 'first floor' level, the platform being reached down a flight of stairs. The structure is in brick, with a half-hipped roof of decorative tiles. The eaves-boards are shaped and pierced, the sash windows are elegantly shaped and a fine glazed canopy is supported on decorative ironwork. The footbridge giving access to the nearer platform emerges from the front elevation at first floor level. *BR*

Left:
A curved cast-iron lattice footbridge (see **Footbridges**) obscures part of the attractive trainshed at Coniston station, terminus of the Furness Railway branch line from Foxfield. The station offices, to the left, are stone-built, as is the main wall on the right, which supports the timber-framed and slated trainshed roof. *LPC/Ian Allan Library*

Right:
Situated on the LNWR branch from Rhyl to Corwen was Ruthin, seen here looking south in June 1949. The line southwards to Corwen closed in 1952 but Rhyl–Ruthin was to remain open for another 10 years. A solid-looking two-storey brick building stands under a slate roof with tall chimney stacks. The canopy has a hipped, glazed section but is otherwise of rather heavy design with thick columns and heavy ironwork supporting an awning with very deep timber valancing. Staff living accommodation was provided on the upper floor. *Real Photographs*

Centre right:
Boasting a standard LMS running in board, Roman Bridge station was a rustic cottage-style structure on the LNWR branch to Blaenau Ffestiniog. Built of stone under a roof of local slate, the mixture of gables and half-hipped roof ends gives a rustic and mellow appearance just right for the area. Even the platform wall is of local stone. The chimneys are grouped into a single large cruciform stack. This, too, was a 1949 view. There was a near-identical building at Pont-y-Pant. *Real Photographs*

Bottom right:
The most basic of the Midland Railway's rural stations were often executed in timber. This example on the Hereford–Three Cocks Junction line was at Whitney-on-Wye and was photographed near the end of its days, in May 1963. Though other stations on the line were also timber, this one differed in having the overhanging eaves on the platform side, forming a rudimentary canopy. The diagonal paling fence (right) is typical of the Midland Railway. *Author's collection*

Left and centre left:
Several of the LNWR stations on the Bletchley–Bedford line employed this mock-Elizabethan 'timber-framed' style and though in poor condition, several of them survive today. Millbrook is currently used as a private dwelling, the station being unstaffed except for the crossing keeper. The great attention to detail includes fretted barge boards (in 4mm scale, Slater's produce a plastic version in similar style and Scalelink does so in etched brass), decorative tiling and fine chimney stacks. *Author*

Below:
The former Midland Railway station at Cardington, seen in 1994, was on the Bedford–Hitchin line, which closed in January 1962 after a short-lived experiment to operate it with Park Royal railbuses (like the Airfix/Dapol 4mm scale model). At one time this rural brick-built station was the embarkation point for hundreds of young men about to start their National Service in the RAF. In the background looms one of the giant airship hangars of RAF Cardington, home of British airships, including the ill-fated R101. *Author*

Above:
Where the railway was in a cutting below street level, stations could sometimes look little different from shop fronts. Here's a classic example in the former London & North Western station at Kilburn. Taken in 1948 as the 'before' view in a series of illustrations of BR improvements, the station boasts its LMS signs. Kemps grocery shop overpowers the station entrance which is hardly discernible on the right beneath a sign obscured by dirt. The marks on the brickwork suggest that the building once had a 'ridge and furrow' glass awning of three sections, while the grocery shop is evidently an example of commercialism where part of the station booking hall has been leased. *BR*

Centre right:
Chalk Farm station, on the North London Railway, in September 1949 before its 'treatment' by BR and being renamed Primrose Hill. Another urban station frontage, this one is executed in red brick with detail in stone and white rendering. Such scenes were typical of the postwar legacy which BR was eager to brighten up as quickly as possible. *BR*

Right:
In connection with the Barking–Upminster electrification in the early 1930s the LMS rebuilt the station at Becontree in the functional modern style of the day. Straight lines are relieved by 'miniature' brickwork around windows and doors. Galvanised metal window frames — widely used at the time — give a light, airy effect through their narrow glazing bars with no hint of how draughty such windows would become in later years. A view taken on 18 September 1932. *Ian Allan Library*

SOUTHERN REGION

Below:
Remotely situated on the North Cornwall line to Wadebridge and Padstow lay Port Isaac Road station, seen here in September 1930. The single-storey section forms the station offices while the remainder is dwelling accommodation for the stationmaster. The building is executed in local granite with the recessed waiting-shelter section having timber storm screens. *Author's collection*

Above:
Clapboard construction in timber was widely used in Kent and was reflected in many of the former South Eastern & Chatham Railway stations. East Farleigh, with its matching signalbox, on the Maidstone–Paddock Wood line, was photographed in 1993 with much NSE equipment in evidence. The timber structures are carried on concrete footings and roofed with corrugated galvanised sheets. Each station door has its own porch in the style of a tiny canopy. The very steep approach to the level crossing seems to have precluded conversion to lifting barriers. *Author*

Above:
Another South Western Railway building, this was Datchet on the Staines–Windsor branch. The single-sto station offices carry a standard LSWR canopy on two c iron columns. Adjoining the far end was a two-storey dwelling house and beyond that, until the 1970s, a timber goods shed. The structure was in yellow and re bricks under a slate roof. The station section was destroyed by an arsonist in the 1980s and rebuilt in a modern style, mainly as shops and offices. *Author*

Below:
A fine surviving example of the work of architect Sir William Tite is seen at Chertsey in January 1995. The Italianate style was achieved by adding extra detail to a fairly standard structure already used elsewhere on the South Western. This raised the 'class' of the structure to suit its locality. Built of yellow bricks under a slate roof it features very fine windows, decorated eaves and handsome chimney stacks. Tite did much work for the London & South Western Railway and its predecessors, including the station at Windsor & Eton Riverside. *Author*

Above:
Detail of the upper-floor windows, eaves and chimney stacks at Sir William Tite's Chertsey station. Sadly, much of Chertsey town centre with which the station was designed to harmonise has been torn down in that relentless quest to modernise everything, which seems to afflict southeast England. *Author*

Left:
The uncompromising Victorian style seen on thousands of houses built in the 19th century was also familiar on many South Western stations, though numbers have been swept away in recent modernisations. One such was Virginia Water, seen here in the late 1960s and completely rebuilt about 10 years later with one of the CLASP sectional structures. The original building — its canopy similar to that at Datchet — was in dark yellow bricks with sash windows. The other platforms had just wooden waiting shelters. *Author*

Above:
At Bideford the local North Devon granite was used under a slate roof for a simple but attractive little station building, seen here derelict in 1969. The platform canopy has gone, but a neat porch over the booking office entrance remains. This building subsequently became a branch of Midland Bank and today has been restored to SR green and cream paintwork as part of the local authority's facilities involving use of the former railway route as a coastal path. *David Bowen*

Centre left:
The Southern Railway was responsible for a great deal of excellent modernisation work, much of it in connection with electrification schemes, though not here at Hastings where the attractive frontage is seen in 1935. This style, also employed at Richmond, Wimbledon and Kingston, bears marked similarity to some of the new cinemas of the period. Brick and concrete are blended in a grand manner on quite a modest-sized structure. *R. A. Crystal/Author's collection*

Left:
Modern 'Southern' architecture from the Network SouthEast era produced this neat steel-framed glass and red-brick structure built at Egham in the 1980s. It provides simple, minimum-space facilities for ticket sales and a waiting room yet avoids the run-down dreariness of the sectional concrete CLASP structures erected in the 1960s and 1970s. *Author*

LIGHT RAILWAYS

Right:
The greatest promoter of light railways in the UK was Colonel Holman F. Stephens. His railways, built under legislation which allowed for cheapness of construction in return for a 25mph maximum speed, brought rail services to rural areas where traffic was insufficient to justify anything better. Stephens' buildings had a family likeness, whether built of timber, corrugated iron or more permanent materials. This is Luckett on the Bere Alston–Callington branch, formerly the Colonel's Plymouth, Devonport & South Western Junction Railway.
Real Photographs

Centre right:
The similar structure at Rolvenden, seen here in 1953, boasts the same style of canopy supported on timber posts. Sadly, this building did not survive into preservation. *B. K. B. Green*

Below:
On the Kent & East Sussex Railway, Stephens' stations survive at Northiam, seen here before restoration, and at Bodiam. Both are clad in corrugated iron, painted cream with brown door and window frames. On the left is one of the Colonel's infamous gents' toilets, an open-air urinal consisting of a trough flushed (weather permitting) by rain water from the adjacent gutter! Northiam has been lovingly restored by the KESR — to modern standards — with new toilets provided in a matching structure built alongside. *Author's collection*

Above:
This view of Chelfham station in 1935, just after closure, shows the tiny wooden lean-to extension added by the Southern Railway. The SR made a range of improvements to its only narrow gauge line during the 1920s and early 1930s but could not justify expenditure on major track renewals which were deemed necessary. The five station buildings all remain in existence though some have been altered substantially. *F. E. Box*

Left:
Not quite a true light railway, but a rural narrow gauge line, the Lynton & Barnstaple Railway served a sparsely-populated tract of North Devon and closed in 1935. Two of the small stations, Bratton Fleming and Chelfham, seen here, were built by the line's contractor and provided only a basic ticket office and waiting room. Local stone was used for construction with diamond-shaped clay tiles and decorative clay ridge tiles. Chelfham had gable ends with decorative bargeboards, while Bratton Fleming had a hipped roof.
LGRP/Real Photographs

Above right:
Jones of Lynton built the Lynton & Barnstaple Railway's 'Nuremburg'-style stations at Blackmoor Gate, Woody Bay and Lynton. These two-storey chalet-style buildings included dwelling accommodation. Lynton is seen here after the Southern Railway had extended the building at the far end and added the parcels office with the double doors on the left in this view.
LGRP/Real Photographs

Centre right:
Woody Bay station was the smallest of the three 'Nuremburg' buildings and is here seen partly boarded up just after closure. Built of local stone under a tiled roof and with tile-hung elevations to the upper storey, this handsome station fetched £425 when sold and, having been a private house, has recently been acquired by the Lynyton & Barnstaple Railway Association for restoration to its original use.
Real Photographs

Bottom right:
White Notley, on the Witham–Braintree branch, was actually a Great Eastern station though with much light railway character, including a tiny wooden building and low platform. This was the view in April 1971 when the line was being worked by DMUs.
J. Rickard

Left:
White Notley transformed, but is it any improvement? Electrification of the Braintree branch caused the station to be rebuilt with standard-height platform, modern lights and waiting shelter as seen here in 1981. Though a modern building has been provided for the crossing keeper, the old hand-operated gates have been retained for the time being. Doubtless they didn't last long. Standard corporate image signs have been used and the shelter is one of those ugly 'vandals' delights' of the period. *J. G. Glover*

EASTERN REGION

Right:
The railway-building boom led to some lines in East Anglia for which there was little justification. One such linked the Wells branch with Wroxham. Its junction with the Wells line necessitated a nearby station and the result was County School, built to serve a short-lived Norfolk County Council boarding school. Left derelict after it closed to passengers, County School has since been restored with minimal alteration to provide as near perfect an example of the sleepy rural station as it is possible to find. Few signs of preservation intrude in this 1994 view of the little red-brick building under a grey slate roof. GER initials are incorporated in the canopy ironwork. *Author*

Left:
A Great Eastern station which still looks the part is seen here at Oulton Broad North in 1994. In fact, the building is occupied by a woodworking shop and rail passengers merely have use of the platform canopy for shelter. Of red brick under a tiled roof, the sash windows with eight small panes sliding over two large panes are similar to those at County School. The decorative canopy valancing is a typical GER pattern. *Author*

Left:
Modernisation has removed much of the original station at Lowestoft Central, but the main booking hall still survives and is being renovated. What the future holds for this side-section of the terminus is unclear but in 1994 it still afforded a glimpse of original features in a once-handsome structure. The semicircular arches, neat dormer section, plain chimney and elegant second floor windows are all noteworthy features. The building is of yellow bricks under a slate roof which has received a modern waterproof covering. *Author*

Below:
Another small intermediate station on the Witham–Braintree branch is Cressing, seen here in 1971 before the branch was electrified and modernised. The small rectangular brick booking office carries a platform canopy supported on three cast-iron columns and with typical GER timber valancing. A small signalbox is provided together with the classic GER level crossing comprising wide single gates hung from tall concrete posts and supported with a lengthy stay-rod. Note the ladder attached to the former oil-lamp post. *J. Rickard*

Above:
Fakenham station, on the Wells branch, is seen here from the road approach. The building includes dwelling accommodation and is part rendered, part clap-board construction under hipped slate roofs. Note the brick chimney stack serving the clapboarded office section, with its very tall chimney pot. Though there was a passing loop here, the station had only a single platform. *Ian Allan Library*

Above:
Seen here, still in a remarkably complete state in 1994 despite being closed since 1968, is Cowbit on the Great Northern & Great Eastern Joint line from Spalding to March. GN styling dominates, with the buildings in dark red bricks with cream string courses under a slate roof. There is only a minimal platform canopy. The signalbox with its part-timber gable ends and elaborate bargeboards, is also in a standard GNR style. *Author*

Right:
The street side of Cowbit station, which included substantial living accommodation in a strongly Victorian building. Note the shallow curved tops to doors and windows and the plain functional chimney stacks. One rear window has been bricked up, apparently after the building ceased to be a station. *Author*

Above:
Another plain, functional station of Great Northern origin was Welwyn North in yellow brick under a grey slate roof and seen here in the mid-1960s. The brickwork betrays evidence of repairs and alterations which have not improved the appearance. A fine gas lamp adorns the brick wall to the left. Modernisation and electrification work has seen the reconstruction of most of the GNR stations between King's Cross and Peterborough. *Ian Allan Library*

Centre right:
Lea Bridge, a Great Eastern station close to London on the Chingford branch is seen here on 1 August 1950 after reconstruction. Extensive and obvious brickwork repairs suggest that this may have been due to wartime damage. Though quite a small building, the use of blind-topped arches and heavy stone quoins gives a grand appearance to what would otherwise have been a characterless structure. *BR*

Right:
Though BR inherited the Kelvedon & Tollesbury branch at Nationalisation, it kept the line running only until 1951. Constructed as a light railway with minimal facilities, it was worked for years by the 'tram' coaches made redundant from the Wisbech & Upwell line. Kelvedon Low Level was the junction with the main line, the main line station being up the footpath to the left of the waiting shelter. It presents an almost perfect prototype for a minimum space model, the low platform being scarcely two coaches long. *R. E. Vincent*

Left:
Like most light railways, the line to Tollesbury was a latecomer, not being opened until 1904. The passenger terminus at Tollesbury is seen here in 1950, looking towards Kelvedon. The low platform has oil lamps and a small timber building. *LGRP/Real Photographs*

Above:
The LNER undertook some interesting station rebuildings, particularly where the York–Northallerton quadrupling of tracks necessitated complete reconstruction of stations. Otterington was one such and is seen here in July 1933. Station and signalbox have been rebuilt in complementary styles, the station having both a ramp and steps for access to the central ticket office. This has a stone portal bearing the station name. The structure is in red bricks and concrete with a tiled roof, the broad eaves being reflected in the signalbox. *Ian Allan Library*

Left:
Raskelf was rebuilt in similar style to Otterington, though the buildings here comprise only a small ticket office and waiting shelters. Metal window frames are employed throughout. The platform is a sectional concrete structure, but the retention of oil lighting seems incongruous. *Ian Allan Library*

Right:
A more striking new look was given to Maryland, a former GER station near Stratford, rebuilt by the LNER and seen here on 9 September 1949. The 'eye-shaped' LNER logos would presumably have been the company's house style had not the railway Nationalisation already been 19 months old by then. The plain block finish and angular design are accentuated by dark-coloured metal window frames and plain tubular railings outside. *BR*

Above:
The station at Earls Colne on the former Colne Valley & Halstead Railway is seen here in BR days, having been rebuilt by the LNER as a substantial little station with dwelling attached. *LGRP/Real Photographs*

Right:
Electrification work on lines out of Liverpool Street continued into the 1960s necessitating reconstruction of stations such as Broxbourne, here seen in January 1965 in modern concrete and brick. Such featureless expanses of masonry are among the most difficult structures to model convincingly. *BR*

Above:
This more pleasing rebuild of Potters Bar station was brought about in 1955 due to the quadrupling of tracks through the old GNR station. Though basically little more than a 'box' with glass doors, the striking modern canopy and 'clerestory' of glass and veined vents lift an otherwise plain little building. *BR*

Left:
The 1962 rebuilding of Colchester, seen here, provided long slender platform buildings ideal for modelling where platform widths are necessarily narrow. A sectional concrete platform carries brick and concrete buildings with a timber-faced awning. A timber band encircles the structure just five bricks above ground level. *BR*

Right:
The interesting 1966 rebuild of Billingham station on Teesside shows a neat brick and glass structure with overhanging flat roof built at street level to serve a single-island platform which is just provided with a small waiting shelter. A concrete footbridge links the two. *BR*

WESTERN REGION

Right:
Early GWR station design owed much to Brunel, for the initial designs were his work, later examples being developed or modified by his assistants. His designs for rural wayside stations included two distinct styles, which for convenience we can classify as 'Italianate' and 'roadside', the latter being his own term. This picture shows Aldermaston, an Italianate-style station distinguished by the broad overhanging eaves which form a canopy on all four sides. A matching waiting shelter was provided on the opposite platform. *Author's collection*

Centre right:
The Italianate waiting shelter at Mortimer station, built of red brick and open-fronted, with just a standard bench seat. The slate-roofed structure has since been restored with original-pattern pantiles. A 4mm-scale kit is available in the Pola range. *Author*

Below:
Mortimer station, the last survivor of Brunel's Italianate-style wayside stations, seen here before its period restoration in the 1980s. At this stage it was unstaffed and boarded up, and had been reroofed with slates. Apart from the overhanging eaves with shaped timber beams, the other distinctive feature is the round-topped arches in groups of three over doors and windows. This building is also available from Pola as a 4mm-scale kit. *Author*

Right:
On the Oxford, Worcester & Wolverhampton Railway, lack of funds forced engineer John Fowler to adapt Brunel's Italianate design for construction in timber, a cheaper material than brick in the Cotswolds. This striking example at Charlbury has its original slate roof, and single round-topped windows. It was extensively renovated in 1979, when this photograph was taken to show the completed work. *BR*

Below:
Fowler's smallest stations on the OWW also followed a basic Brunel plan and were executed in timber as seen here at Chipping Campden. One of the most delightful country stations, it had oil lighting until closure in the mid-1960s. The most obvious Brunel feature is the massive stone chimney stack, Campden being the only example to retain this feature throughout. None of these timber stations, which once existed at Adlestrop, Handborough and Ascott-under-Wychwood, among others, now survive. *Author's collection*

Left:
Though the GWR had many 'standard' buildings, there were far more non-standard ones and many which included some familiar features in an otherwise unusual structure. Here is Midgham, in an official 1946 view. A plain rectangular building with typical timber canopy valancing, it is clearly of early design, featuring fine traditional chimney stacks and the same pattern of cast-iron canopy brackets found on Brunel's 'roadside' station at Culham. Midgham was reduced to basic shelters as an unstaffed halt in the 1960s. *BR/Author's collection*

Right:
Though boarded up and near the end of its career, there is no mistaking Brunel's influence in the handsome waiting shelter at Stonehouse — just look at that Italianate stone chimney stack. The flat canopy on cast-iron brackets is a development of the 'roadside' stations and the structure is built of stone under a slate roof. At the height of its 'careless' era, in the mid-1970s, BR mounted a successful campaign to demolish all the original structures at Stonehouse despite their DoE 'listed' Grade II status. *Author*

Above:
Brunel's design for the station at Box was reproduced in a slightly amended form at several sites between Oxford and Banbury. This is Aynho for Deddington, now the only survivor of the type. (The similar building at Heyford was dismantled by the Great Western Society and moved to Didcot but not yet re-erected.) The waiting shelter on the right was markedly similar to that at Stonehouse. *LGRP/Real Photographs*

Right:
Aynho station last served as a coal office . It is shown standing derelict in 1993 shortly before it was converted to a private dwelling. In my view this was the finest of all GWR country station types. *Author*

Below:
The semicircular arches and Italianate chimneys from the Brunel style have been retained in this red-brick structure at Marlow, but the shape is now unquestionably a railway station. A single-storey structure with a modest canopy supported on cast-iron brackets, it had a slate roof. Note the screen at the nearer end, around the gents' toilet entrance. The timber screen is supported on cast-iron columns similar to those used by the GWR for its station nameboards. *Ian Allan Library*

Below:
From the Danks design was developed the rectangular station building in which doors, windows, skylights, rainwater goods and all details were standardised across a range of broadly similar structures. These were usually built of red bricks with blue engineers' bricks used for decoration on plinths, quoins (corners), and window reveals to varying extents. A hipped slate roof was normal, as seen here at Badminton in the 1960s. *Keith Willows*

Above:
The next step in the development of 'standard' GWR architecture was the development of a design by J. E. Danks featuring a French colonial styling with 'turrets' topped with spiky cast ironwork. It was at its most lavish at Slough but there were smaller examples at stations such as Ross-on-Wye and here at Stourbridge Town. This building was in pale cream bricks with red and blue string courses and with curved stone window lintels topped by coloured bricks which were to become a feature of GWR buildings in the later years of the 19th century. A canopy of glass and corrugated iron is supported on steel trusses and cast-iron columns employing the same 'fasces' decoration of bound reeds used by Brunel. *Author*

Above:
A view of the down side building at Savernake Low Level during demolition in about 1968 shows the steel-framed canopy used with these late 19th-century GWR buildings. With the rear slope glazed and the front portion clad in corrugated iron, the canopy is carried on steel trusses bracketed from the wall and devoid of pillars. This structure contained a waiting room and toilets. *Author*

Above:
An unusual variation of the 'standard' GWR building was achieved at Castle Cary by blending an early stone-built rectangular Brunelian building with a later-style canopy. An excellent plastic kit of this building is available to 4mm:1ft-scale modellers in the Ratio range. *Author*

Centre right:
In the final development of the standard station design, the rectangular red-brick building was constructed as a simple 'box' with a flat concrete roof. A steel-framed canopy, glazed and clad in corrugated iron, was constructed with its peak above the front of the station building. Wootton Bassett, built in the early 20th century and seen here on 14 October 1966 was typical. Since the canopy was easily removed, the few structures which survive have generally lost their canopies. However, a fine preserved example exists at Toddington. *K. Willows*

Right:
The arrangement of the canopy over the complete flat-roofed structure can be seen in this old view of Winscombe. This design was ideal for more urban stations where small buildings were required under large expanses of canopy, as for instance at Tyseley. *Author*

Left:
Many and varied were the non-standard structures which the GWR inherited from its constituent companies. The Berks & Hants Extension Railway was responsible for this fine red-brick station at Savernake Low Level, designed to match the adjacent Forest Hotel. The GWR erected the down platform and its standard waiting room. *R. J. Leigh*

Above:
A very small version of the BHER building was employed at Bedwyn. It featured the same decorative coloured brickwork and stone quoins as at Savernake. *Real Photographs*

Right:
In contrast, the largest of the BHER buildings, and the only one still standing, was at Pewsey, seen here in about 1965. Splendid gables, porches, stone quoins and decoration are featured. *Author*

Left:
Neen Sollars, on the Bewdley–Tenbury Wells branch was typical of stations inherited by the GWR in that area, and similar to those on the nearby Severn Valley line. A small station office with canopy on the platform side, and an attached dwelling with a Victorian bay window form the only structure. The opposite platform has only a basic waiting shelter. *LGRP/Ian Allan Library*

Right:
Buildwas Junction station building was an enlarged version of the Severn Valley standard type, built in yellow bricks under a slate roof. Two gable wings, one a single-storey office and the other a double-storey dwelling were joined by a single-storey section with canopy, containing the booking office and waiting room. Buildwas, however, lacked the distinctive bay window which made the neighbouring stations rather more attractive. *LGRP/Ian Allan Library*

Left:
The GWR inherited from the Witney Railway wooden stations at Eynsham, seen here, and South Leigh, together with another at Witney which had been converted to a goods office when the East Gloucestershire Railway extended the branch to Fairford. In the BR period, when this view was taken, the wooden building wore a faded blue/green and cream colour scheme which the WR had applied to several stations in the area. The left-hand, down platform was a GWR sectional concrete structure erected during World War 2. It has since been moved to Didcot Railway Centre and re-erected to serve the demonstration line there. *Ian Allan Library*

Left:
The GWR did not acquire the Midland & South Western Junction Railway until 1923. This is the MSWJR station at Cricklade seen in the GWR period. It was a single-storey red-brick structure under a grey slate roof, having a substantial platform canopy supported on cast-iron columns. The MSWJR produced a mixture of station buildings including structures in timber (Chedworth) and Cotswold stone (Cirencester Watermoor). *LGRP/Ian Allan Library*

ht:
the Lambourn Valley way the GWR erited a number of und-level halts which eplaced with its own ctures. It also rebuilt Lambourn terminus n a standard red-brick 2' station. Speen, n here, was provided n a timber-faced tform and a ugated iron goda'-style waiting lter produced in kit n by Joseph Ash & s of Birmingham. The ic ticket office may l have been original. one from Welford k is preserved at cot Railway Centre. *l Photographs*

Left:
The East Gloucestershire Railway terminus at Fairford seen at an unknown date in GWR days. The single-storey stone station building did not include dwelling accommodation and was similar to those at Lechlade and Brize Norton, and the brick-built example at Alvescot. The stone goods shed is also original but the signalbox and 'pagoda' cycle shed are GWR additions. In the right foreground are sheds for platelayers' trolleys, the straggling 25-mile branch from Oxford requiring mechanised transport for permanent way staff.
Author's collection

Left:
At Carbis Bay, on the St Ives branch, the single-storey granite station building was set at street level, with the platform in a cutting below. A GWR waiting shelter similar to those at Cookham and Colnbrook, among others, was provided on the platform. The station was demolished before 1966 and has been an unstaffed halt ever since.
Author's collection

Centre left:
Colnbrook station was unique in its styling, being the only station built by the Staines & West Drayton Railway (its terminus at Staines being converted from an extant private house). Colnbrook was built of dark yellow bricks with red string courses and some quite elaborate detailing in terracotta tiles. The platform canopy was timber-framed with stout timber braces to the wall between each pair of windows. An unusual feature in its later years was the provision of a 'mousehole' ticket window on to the platform, there being no booking hall as most of the building had been converted into a dwelling for railway staff. *Author's collection*

Below:
A delightful railway curiosity was Black Dog halt on the Chippenham–Calne branch, until 1952 a private station for adjacent Bowood House. When the station was built Lord Lansdowne had erected 'a shed, for the sum of £55'. The nameplate was added when BR finally took it over in 1952. At the right-hand end, a join is clearly visible where the structure has been extended at some time, this end being the ticket office and the other a parcels room. The branch closed in 1965 and Black Dog halt was demolished by Douglas Lovelock, its last stationmaster.
Don Lovelock

Above:
St Ives station was a compact terminus with a long platform squeezed on a shelf above Porthminster beach. This 1920s view is looking towards St Erth. A stiff climb faced departing trains, necessitating double-heading of some trains, while on summer Saturdays during the 1950s the through 'Cornish Riviera' stock would be double-headed by 2-6-2Ts and banked in the rear by a third member of the class. *Author's collection*

Below:
By 1966 St Ives station had been rationalised to single track and was operated by a single diesel railcar. The authorities had been confident of closure under Beeching but the line was officially reprieved due to severe traffic congestion in the summer. A successful park and ride scheme gave the line a new lease of life, but not before the handsome granite station had been totally erased and replaced by a scruffy new halt slightly further up the line. The station area is now a car park. *Author*

Left:
The exterior of the rugged granite station at St Ives. Stone arches link windows and doors and the accommodation is designed to deal with the summer influx of passengers and with a large traffic in fish from the adjacent goods shed. The roof was of local slate. *S. W. Stevens-Stratten*

Centre left:
Famed as the setting for Titfield in *The Titfield Thunderbolt* this is Monkton Combe station on the Limpley Stoke–Camerton branch in 1947, five years before the filming. The little rustic station building in timber has had corrugated asbestos weatherproofing added to the end. It probably presents the most ideal prototype for a small model layout. *Author's collection*

SCOTTISH REGION

Right:
The builders of the West Highland line made extensive use of concrete, as in the platform face seen here. The stations on this section were usually island platforms, often reached by a subway under the line and having these distinctive buildings with the curved hip roof producing wide overhanging eaves. At each end there were glazed weather screens. In this view of Bridge of Orchy, the nearer building is the former signalbox, disused in this 1991 view. Bridge of Orchy is unusual in that the station building also incorporates the village Post Office. *Author*

Right:
The curved hip roof with broad eaves also featured in some Highland Railway buildings as in this very attractive example at Nairn — no longer used as a station but leased privately. Built of shiplapped timbers, it is a rugged, simple structure, yet manages to be elegant. The roof is slate with stone chimney stacks. *Author*

Left:
A rather more simple, ordinary structure of featheredge boarding was provided by the Glasgow, Barrhead & Kilmarnock Railway (Glasgow & South Western and Caledonian Joint) at Beith, terminus of the branch from Lugton. Note the way in which the ends of the rafters form a row under the eaves, and also the cast-iron drinking fountain at the nearer end of the building. Traffic on this little branch line, southwest of Glasgow, was sufficiently light to prompt its operation by railbus in the 1960s, and AC Cars diesel railbus No Sc79979 can be seen at the platform in this May 1960 view. *J. N. Faulkner*

Right:
Built in similar style to its West Highland neighbour, the Invergarry and Fort Augustus Railway was an impecunious private scheme with big ideas. It was not completed until the early years of the present century, leased to the Highland Railway, closed, leased to the North British Railway, closed again in 1911, reopened and finally closed by the LNER in 1934 to passengers and in 1946 to goods. With its wide draught screens seen here, Invergarry echoed the West Highland's island-platform arrangement but with a simpler timber and stucco building. In its early years the station had an awning extending over the track on one side to provide weatherproof facilities for the rich and famous coming to hunt and shoot on the Invergarry Estate. *Real Photographs*

STATION HOUSES

MANY railway companies, large and small, provided living accommodation for staff and sometimes, as at Tebay, whole communities grew up around what began as a railway installation. The dwellings would vary from tiny cottages for crossing keepers, through terraced Victorian dwellings for the workers in railway factories, to quite substantial detached homes for stationmasters. The Great Western was still building such properties in the 1920s and, indeed, in an effort to encourage staff into the London suburbs there was a considerable drive to provide extra dwellings in the 1930s. This was achieved in part by converting surplus rooms in station buildings and was successful in tempting many a Welsh railwayman into the West London suburbs, where their families remain.

Above:
A truly classic GWR stationmaster's house is this example at Adlestrop. It is built in alternating courses of red bricks and engineers' blues, so beloved of the GWR, under a grey slate roof and is to a 'standard' outline found at many other places. Even so, the only obvious railway features are the cream chimney pots and the GWR picket fence to the left. In GWR days the paintwork colour for domestic buildings was dark green. These houses were provided as part of the GWR improvements to stations on the Oxford, Worcester & Wolverhampton Railway route. *Author*

Right:
The stationmaster's house at Savernake (Low Level). The design apparently dates from around 1912, in red brick and roughcast rendering under a tiled roof. Most such houses are now in private ownership, the stations for which they were built having long gone. *Author*

Left:
Various buildings at Cowbit on the Great Northern & Great Eastern Joint line north of Peterborough have been covered in this volume. The site is unusual in that virtually all the structures survive so long after closure and this is a 1994 view of what is obviously a railway house, situated just across the road from the station. The railway trackbed runs in the foreground of this view and there was a level crossing here. Since the station building contained its own dwelling accommodation, this is probably the crossing keeper's house, many GER-type level crossings being worked by hand even where (as at Cowbit) there was a substantial signalbox nearby. *Author*

TABLET CATCHERS

TO regulate traffic and operate safely over single lines a system of tokens or tablets was derived. These took the form of either a staff, a large key or a flat metal ring which fitted into an instrument in the signalbox. In order to traverse a section of single line, the driver had to be in possession of the token for that section. A token could only be released from the instrument with the co-operation of the signalman at the far end of the section, the instruments being electrically interlocked. This ensured that only one token could be issued at a time and, therefore, that one train only was in the section.

On long single-line routes with passing places, where tokens would need to be exchanged when moving from one section to the next, exchanges could take place by hand between footplateman and signalman. However, faster operation and nonstop trains required something more sophisticated.

On some lines — notably on the GWR — token-exchange apparatus was provided close to the signalbox. The token was clipped to a large hoop and placed in position atop a post so that the fireman could collect it by putting his arm through the hoop as he passed. He delivered the token at the end of the section by hooking the hoop over a metal arm attached to a lineside post. The arm would be backed by a net or board for good measure, just in case he missed!

On some other lines, the Whitaker automatic tablet exchanger was used. Mainly used with the round tablets, this system required less precision from the train crew. The tablet was placed in a leather pouch attached to a metal ring and placed in a pivoted arm on the lineside apparatus. A forked arm below this was swung out ready to pick up the tablet from the engine. On approaching the exchange point, the fireman would suspend the tablet in its pouch from an arm which swung out from the side of the cab or tender. As the lineside apparatus snatched the token in its forked arm, so a similar device on the engine would pick up the new tablet. The train did not need to slow down for this system, while the GWR arrangement carried 15mph speed limit signs.

Right:
The GWR system at Colnbrook. The picking up post can be seen to the left of the autocoach, this being a post-1920 installation with tubular steel post. Note the board crossing and wooden step for the signalman. The setting-down apparatus to the right of the train is an older wooden post installation. Oil lamps were provided to illuminate both pieces of apparatus for night operation. Wooden posts were painted white with black bases and metal posts were painted silver.
E. R. Wethersett/Ian Allan Library

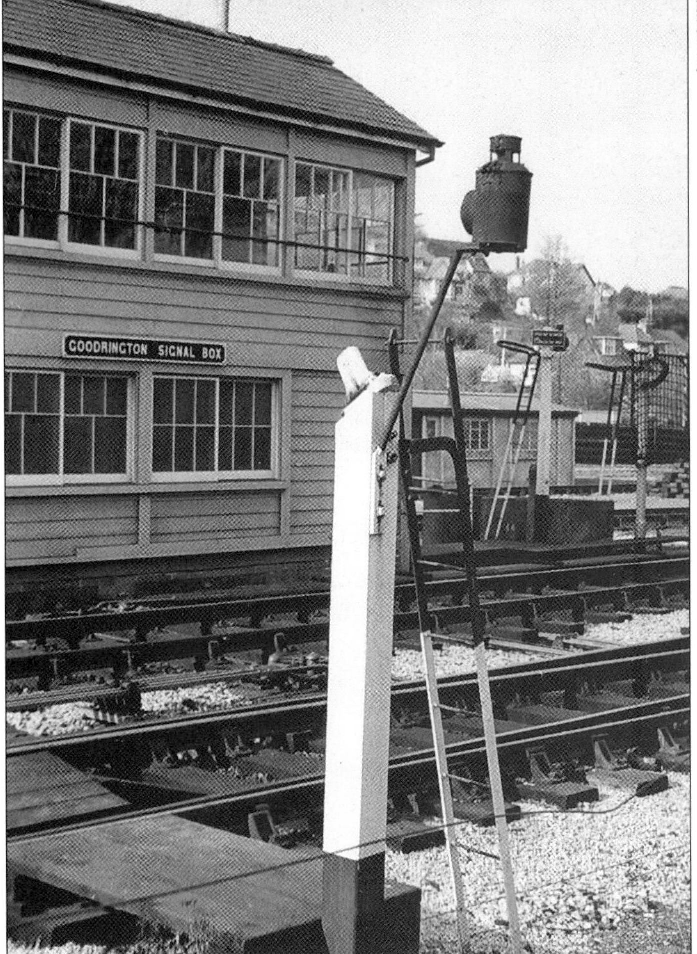

Left:
A close-up of a GWR wooden-post installation at Goodrington on the Kingswear line. The token hoop fits into the cast-iron arrangement on the angled head of the post. The metal ladder and oil lamp were usual. *Ian Allan Library*

Right:
The setting-down apparatus at Goodrington shows clearly how the oil lamp was carried on a separate post together with a 15mph speed limit warning. The set-down apparatus here has the tubular metal post with the obligatory metal ladder. On some old wooden-post equipment the net was replaced by a white-painted board and the hooked arm was bound in leather.
Ian Allan Library

Left:
The Whitaker automatic equipment at Crossmichael station in Scotland. Both picking up and setting down were performed simultaneously by the same piece of apparatus. Here, the tablet is in place in its pouch on the upper arm. The lower arm will receive the incoming tablet from the locomotive. *Ian Allan Library*

Below:
The moment of exchange. The jaws of the locomotive arm snatch the tablet as the incoming pouch is just a blur, swinging in the upper hook of a Whitaker apparatus on the Midland & Great Northern Joint line. The handle and bevel gear enabled the signalman to rotate the arm without having to go too close to the line. *Ian Allan Library*

Above:
The Whitaker apparatus with two pouches in place at the moment of exchange, in a stationary posed photograph on the Somerset & Dorset Joint line. Apart from the S&D and the M&GN, a number of single track routes in Scotland were equipped with this system and it lasted into the diesel era, a number of first generation diesel locomotives being fitted with exchangers on the cab sides. *Ian Allan Library*

Above:
The locomotive equipment, seen retracted, shows clearly the receiving (large) and setting down (small) jaws of the Whitaker system. *Ian Allan Library*

Above:
The Whitaker lineside equipment at Binegar on the Somerset & Dorset, showing the cast-iron post and the handle arrangement for swinging the operating arm into position. *Ian Allan Library*

TICKET MACHINES

TICKET machines on British railways, other than London Underground, are a recent phenomenon and strictly for the modern-image modeller. They have only been possible since engineers have managed to produce a machine which could distinguish genuine banknotes from any other sort of paper. First introduced on Network SouthEast so that tickets could be purchased when stations were not staffed, they have since spread to any locations where ticket offices are unstaffed at certain times when trains are still running.

Right:
The standard self-service ticket machine introduced by Network SouthEast in the 1980s is a simple rectangular unit with a narrow visor to keep the worst of the weather off its numerous push-buttons. The machines can be installed outside, under platform canopies or inside station booking halls. NSE machines are usually Network Red on an aluminium plinth. A 4mm-scale casting for one of these machines is included in the Chris Leigh accessories range. *Author*

TRACK

SURPRISINGLY little has been written about railway track from a modelling viewpoint, probably because most modellers buy their track in ready-made sections or flexible lengths, fix it down, ballast it and get on with the more interesting aspects of modelling. Nevertheless, correctly detailed track does add greatly to the impression of realism. In this section I have included a small selection of photographs showing a few details of this one essential feature of all layouts.

Though early track employed stone sleepers, wood quickly became the norm until prewar experiments with steel sleepers and soon afterwards with concrete. Convincing ballast, a correct cess and accurately constructed points and crossings are other features necessary for realistic trackwork.

Above:
Plain track on the main line at Langley, GWR, in 1946 shows the use of flat-bottom rail with spring clips to cast baseplates on wooden sleepers. This is the up fast line, the only one in this view to have been relaid with flat-bottom rails. The down fast (left) retains its bullhead rails set in chairs with wooden keys. The rails are jointed in 60ft lengths with fishplates having four bolts — welding was not then in use. Flat-bottom rail on wooden sleepers is standard for flexible track in various scales and gauges from Peco and other manufacturers. *BR*

Above:
A view of newly-installed jointed flat-bottom rail at Alne on the North Eastern Region of BR in 1949. The rail is of 109lb/yd weight which was the standard for BR flat-bottom rail for many years. The new ballast shows clearly the very high quality of British tracklaying — what the Americans would call 'manicured track' with the cess at the left clearly defined. The ballast shoulder and cess are designed to facilitate drainage. The wires across the fishplate (centre) are electrical bonding for track circuits. *BR*

Below:
Outside Waterloo station in 1936 we see traditional bullhead rail in cast chairs on wooden sleepers, all newly installed with the added complication of the SR conductor rail for its 750V dc electric trains. The conductor rail is flat-bottom and in this view of complex points and crossings much of it is shielded by timber guards to reduce the risks to staff. In addition, the sharp curve on the extreme left has a check rail inside the running rail to minimise the risk of derailment. Large amounts of power and signal cabling can be seen on and beside the left-hand wall. *SR/Ian Allan Library*

Left:
An unusual feature of the track at this unknown Southern Railway location in November 1942 is the movable point frog in which the frog-ends of the switch rail close to provide a continuous rail surface. In this view the left-hand flangeway has been closed. This arrangement provided a smoother ride and less wear to the point frog, but to the best of my knowledge has not been readily available in model pointwork as it has never found widespread use on BR. *SR/Ian Allan Library*

Below:
Probably the ultimate track complex in a small space is the 'scissors crossover', which allows complete versatility for trains to cross between two parallel lines in either direction. It is at its most useful, as here at Liverpool Street, in allowing up and down services to use two platforms from either line. This March 1962 view shows a new installation of flat-bottom rail on wooden sleepers but using manganese steel crossings in order to withstand the tremendous pounding that such a crossover would take. Tracks in the background and foreground retain their old bullhead rails. *BR*

Below:
Track rationalisation in the late 1960s is causing this Somerset section to lose its relief lines. The main line on which the 'Warship' diesel is travelling has been laid in long-welded flat-bottom rails on concrete sleepers — the railway's latest standard. Just ahead of the locomotive is an expansion joint where four wooden sleepers with short rail lengths attached join two sections of up to $1\frac{1}{4}$ miles of continuous rail. The running rails have tapered joints which permit movement when the rail expands in hot weather. *Author*

Left:
Traditional bullhead track sections being laid, secondhand, at Cory's siding, Staines, in 1981 in connection with a rail diversion for the M25 motorway. Points to note include the new ballast shoulder, earthworks and fencing, concrete cable ducting and the piecemeal construction of the curve from the SR line. *Author*

Right:
A turn-out (in model terms, a right-hand point) in flat-bottom rail on a traditional branch line. Note the check rails, and the way in which vegetation has crept over the cess, due to general lack of maintenance. *Author*

Left:
Another traditional branch line, seen in the 1950s with bullhead rails and timber sleepers. '57XX' 0-6-0PT No 3682 is leaving Black Dog halt with the 5.36pm Calne–Chippenham. The siding to the left of the engine is protected by a catch point — a simple device which is set to derail any wagon which might run away towards the 'main' line. The adjacent ground signal operates in conjunction with the turn-out on to the main line. All the points and the ground signal were operated from a ground frame cabin. *Don Lovelock*

Right:
Steel sleepers are hard wearing and have been used successfully in many locations since prewar times. This is a 1970s installation with flat-bottom rails held in Pandrol clips. This jointed track has been laid in position but not yet ballasted. *BR*

Left:
Concrete sleepers dating from GWR days and with chaired bullhead rails are seen here on the Gloucester–Hereford (via Ross-on-Wye) line *c*1964. These early concrete sleepers are recognisable by the distinctive shape of the depressed centre section. The ballast shoulder and cess can be seen. *Author*

Right:
A modern right-hand turn-out in flat-bottom rails on new timber sleepers with cast baseplates and Pandrol clips is about to be pounded by two Class 37 locomotives and the Port Talbot–Llanwern iron ore train, at that time Britain's heaviest train. Note the perfect, level ballasting and, in contrast, the rather less neat trunking on the right. *BR*

TROLLEYS

THE station porter's trolley for moving parcels and passengers' baggage has been around since the dawn of rail travel. Usually these trolleys were so well made that they lasted for many years and dozens of Victorian trolleys and barrows survived on railway stations into the 1960s. Even nowadays it is possible to find the odd elderly barrow at a wayside station, although these days such items have usually been retired to a merely decorative role.

Above:
A classic Southern Region porter's barrow, possibly of London & South Western Railway origin. There were older versions with spoked wooden wheels. *Frank Crudass*

Above:
A sturdy four-wheeled barrow with pivoted front axle is seen at Stockport in the 1970s, loaded with a tea urn and catering trolley to be used on a Manchester–Birmingham express. This old barrow is probably of London & North Western Railway origin. *D. Birch*

Below:
A vintage Midland Railway barrow still in use at St Pancras in the 1950s. The trolley has a timber main frame with slatted metal deck and end and very crude spoked metal wheels with no tyres of any sort. An identical trolley was still in use at Appleby in 1984! *BR*

Right:
An electric elevating platform truck at Tyneside Central Freight Depot in 1963. The vehicle is battery powered and has a platform which can be raised and lowered for moving stillages (early pallets). *BR*

Left:
An altogether different type of trolley is represented by this mobile snack bar on the concourse of one of the London termini in the 1950s. The whole unit is mounted on giant castors and has a front handrail to assist in manoeuvring it. *BTC*

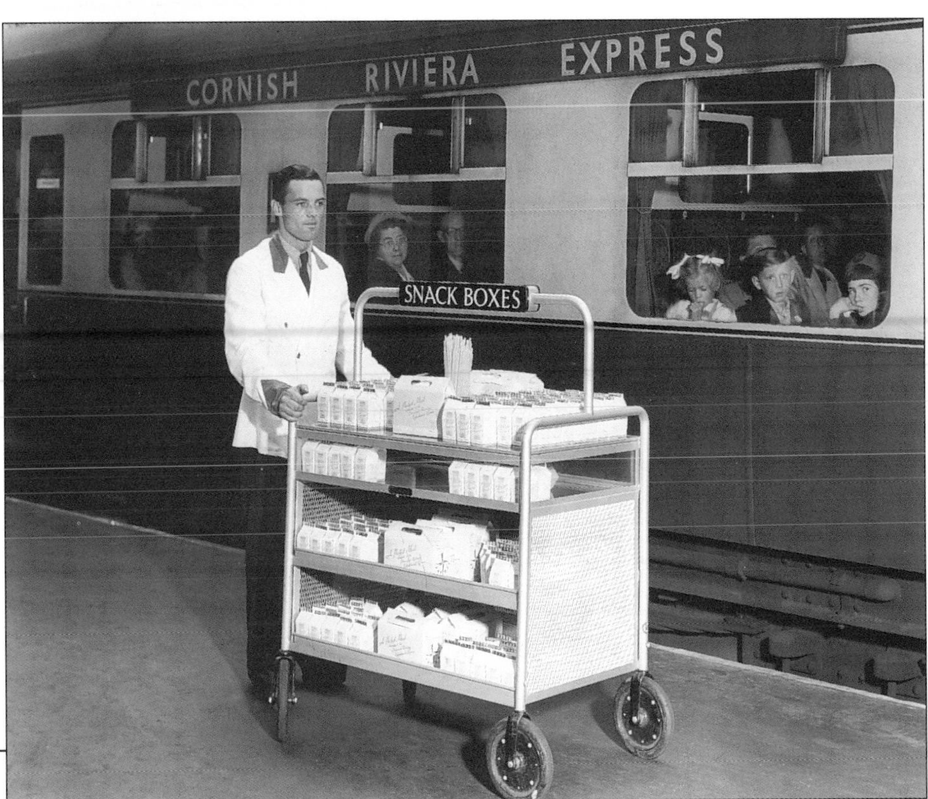

Right:
Photographed in connection with the 1951 Festival of Britain, this catering trolley which roamed the platforms at Paddington was selling Festival-branded drinks and snack boxes for consumption on the train. It would be many more years before such facilities were routinely provided on expresses. *BR*

Above:
The modern on-train catering trolley is quite an important feature for even a medium-sized model station. Most of these on-train trolley services are franchised to small catering companies who change crews, reload and restock their trolleys at stations en route — a perfect scene to recreate on a model. Such facilities are by no means restricted to InterCity services, as many cross-country Sprinter trains now have trolley catering. *Ian Allan Library*

Below:
A standard Great Western Railway platform luggage barrow seen on a preserved line. This barrow retains its original branding showing that it was allocated to Chipping Sodbury station. Such barrows were to be found at all ex-GWR stations well into the 1970s, only being replaced by the BR 'BRUTE' and the modern airport-style luggage trolleys. A plastic kit in 4mm scale is available from Coopercraft. *Author*

Below:
Ranks of BR's universal trolleys (better known as 'BRUTES') are loaded at Peterborough in July 1970 with parcels being despatched from the Freemans mail order business. These trolleys were a feature of stations and parcels depots throughout the country and were also for ease of loading and unloading on to trains. *British Rail*

TUNNEL PORTALS

Above:
The familiar eastern portal of Brunel's Box Tunnel of bricks with stone facings and the distinctive 'fasces' — a classical decoration based on a bundle of reeds bound together which Brunel also used in cast-iron canopy columns. 'King' 4-6-0 No 6000 *King George V* is emerging from the tunnel in this June 1927 publicity photograph. *GWR/Ian Allan Library*

THE builders of Britain's railways expended much time, thought and expense in ensuring that their grand schemes made an impact and that they would be seen as the bold ventures they were. The result, in station buildings and bridges, was some spectacular architecture and gems of design which are still highly regarded 150 years later. Tunnel mouths, or portals, also provided an opportunity for bold architectural statements. Classical styles were imitated for structures in brick or stone, designed to frame the locomotives of the day.

Left:
At Box, Wiltshire, Brunel produced two tunnels, Box and Middle Hill, with different styles of portal. The essential feature, seen here, was an opening far higher than it needed to be. This high opening was a perfect frame for the tall-chimneyed broad-gauge locomotives. Curved stone retaining walls flank the western portal of Box Tunnel, which has a stone balustrade along the top. This is an early view in the standard-gauge period but the tunnel portal remains the same today, with IC125s passing through it. *Real Photographs*

Centre left:
An altogether different style was used by the Midland Railway for this portal of Totley Tunnel, dated 1893. Stone construction is used throughout, though a brick lining would be employed inside the tunnel. Note the ring of shaped stones around the opening, with the keystone bearing the 'MR' initials. The wing walls here are short and straight but, because of the deep cutting, are set at an angle to the portal. There are stone cappings to the portal and wing walls.
Ian Allan Library

Below:
The grand stone portal of Primrose Hill Tunnel on the LMR frames an English Electric Type 1 diesel No D8017 in the late 1950s. Massive stone columns flank the tunnel portal from which six 'gargoyle' heads stare down. The curved brick-built wing walls are buttressed with stone columns with elaborate curved stone caps. The portal has been blackened by years of soot accumulation. *BR*

Right:
A plain and simple brick portal with a near-circular opening was employed for the single-line bore at Colwall, Herefordshire, where the main line reduces to single track in order to economise on the tunnel. Here, the right wing wall is parallel to the portal, while the smaller left one is angled outwards. Note the rings of bricks around the opening. *F. A. Haynes*

Left:
Fairburn 2-6-4T No 42099 emerges from the short tunnel between Oxted and Hurst Green on the Southern Region in 1952. Eight rings of brickwork form the tunnel lining, visible around the aperture, while the rest is fairly plain brickwork with stone cappings. The left-hand wing wall is in a poor state, many of the soft bricks seeming to have fallen out. *C. R. L. Coles*

Below left:
Pylle Tunnel, on the Avonmouth branch near Bristol, shows a basic and uninspired portal, consistent with a builder trying to economise. Local stone forms the portal and the retaining wall for what could easily have been a deeper cutting, but was probably the result of a local landowner insisting that the line had to be hidden. There were a number of such tunnels in the UK where lines passed close to the homes of unsympathetic landowners, and they provide an ideal excuse for including a tunnel on a layout where the scenic terrain does not warrant one. *LGRP/Real Photographs*

Right:
In this 1983 photograph BR was (and still is) using the 1839 Pontardulais tunnel, originally built for horse-drawn traffic. A very small portal in rough stone frames a Central Wales line DMU. A variety of plastic tunnel portals are available in OO and N scales from manufacturers such as Peco and Wills. *BR*

Left:
An unusual peaked portal is a feature of Bopeep Tunnel on the former South Eastern Railway. The fairly plain brick portal frames an opening which is half an ellipse — a most distinctive arrangement. Again, the wing walls are parallel with the portal. *LGRP/Real Photographs*

Right:
Chipping Campden Tunnel on the Oxford, Worcester & Wolverhampton Railway, between Moreton-in-Marsh and Evesham, boasts an unusual curved brick portal with stone facing around the aperture. Brunel was involved with this railway, but much of the design work was done by John Fowler.
Real Photographs

Left:
Cotswold stone features heavily in the retaining walls and bridges leading up to Sapperton Tunnel whose simple stone portal is seen here. The aperture has straight side walls and a shallow elliptical top. *Real Photographs*

Below:
The whole of Littleborough Summit Tunnel can be seen in this view. The Lancashire & Yorkshire Railway tunnel features a stone portal and lining with matching wing walls. Note the extensive walling above the tunnel and the piles of stone used to retain the ground above the portal. *H. Weston*

TURNTABLES

THE means of turning locomotives on a balanced and pivoted 'table' or bridge was developed from wagon turntables which were used, with shunting horses, to enable wagons to reach into industrial premises where no other means of access could be provided.

Locomotive turntables — usually manufactured by engineering firms such as Ransomes & Rapier or Stothert & Pitt — came in sizes from around 40ft up to 70ft to take the longest tender engines. They could be hand-operated by pushing, or by winding crank handles, but the larger and more modern ones operated by vacuum using a hose linked to the locomotive's vacuum brake pipe. The larger examples were generally at motive power depots or close to major termini, but many a rural branch line terminus could boast its own more modest turntable.

Below:
A simple wagon turntable in an industrial setting, which enabled a single wagon to be turned to enter premises it could not otherwise have reached. The table deck is timber with a large iron pivot bearing in the centre. Some scenic ranges such as Langley Models include wagon turntables in their range. *M. Andress*

Below:
A row of four wagon turntables provide links from separate sidings into the warehouse building at Heaton Norris goods depot of the London & North Western Railway, still in use in this 1957 view. The movement would be made by a shunting locomotive using a rope passed around one of the capstans. *T. Lewis*

Left:
The fireman is turning Ivatt 2-6-2T No 41224 by hand outside the little terminus engine shed at Swanage in May 1966. He can be seen pushing hard to the right of the front buffers. This little turntable, just long enough for the usual branch tank engine, has been fully reinstated by the Swanage Railway at this preserved station. *J. Scrace*

Right:
Standard '4MT' 2-6-0 No 76013 is ready for turning at Eastleigh motive power depot in August 1963, on a typical medium-sized turntable. In this example the girders are above track level and run on four wheels set on a ring of rail. Other types had girders beneath the track level and the structure set in a circular pit. *J. Scrace*

Left:
Hughes-Fowler 'Crab' 2-6-0 No 42918 is to be turned at Dumfries on the vacuum-operated turntable. This example has underhung girders set in a pit. Model turntables in N and OO gauges are available from Peco, while an inexpensive OO-gauge kit is included in the Dapol range. *T. G. Hepburn*

UNLOADING
(see also Cranes)

ONE special unloading facility is featured here because it does not fit the other categories — the china clay unloading operation at Fowey.

Above:
At Carne Point, on the Lostwithiel–Fowey branch, the GWR built extensive plant for unloading the end-door china clay wagons and transferring the load into waiting ships. Here, a wagon is tipped on the tilting platform to deliver its load into underground conveyors. A 1964 view. *BR*

VIADUCTS

(see also Arches/Bridges)

FEW layouts are large enough to feature a full-size viaduct but nevertheless some fine model viaducts have been built and occasionally a layout includes a viaduct as its central feature, as on the Dartmoor Scene at Pendon Museum, which features a timber viaduct.

If you are choosing to model a major viaduct then there are a number of helpful books available and drawings should be sought if possible. Many examples of bridges and viaducts are featured in *British Railway Bridges & Viaducts* by Martin Smith; published by Ian Allan.

The following is merely a selection of typical styles.

Above:
Not all viaducts have to be tall. Across the Eton marshland beside the Thames, Brunel built the Windsor–Slough branch on a timber trestle which soon had to be replaced by a long string of brick arches. In May 1963 'Jubilee' 4-6-0 No 45562 *Alberta* was photographed crossing the Brunel bowstring girder bridge over the Thames and heading on to the long viaduct which forms much of the 2½ miles to Slough.
G. T. Robinson

Right:
On the climb to Sapperton, Gloucestershire, the fine brick viaduct at Frampton Mansell is still a much-admired feature. 'Grange' 4-6-0 No 6866 *Morfa Grange* is heading uphill, banked in the rear by a '41XX' class 2-6-2T. Note the buttress to the brickwork beyond the farthest arch.
B. J. Ashworth

Right:
A breakdown train propels gently over Pinmore Viaduct, Glasgow & South Western Railway, in September 1962. The viaduct is of stone with concrete arches and a metal parapet railing. The pier below the locomotive tender has been tied around with bands of metal to reinforce the stonework which is probably suffering from water/frost damage. *Derek Cross*

Below:
Made to look like stone blocks, the viaduct at Calstock, Cornwall, over the River Tamar is an example of early use of concrete for major civil engineering work. A splendid design, with tapered piers and a finely detailed parapet, it carries the Gunnislake branch from Devon into Cornwall and is the first crossing of the Tamar above Saltash. *C. Mogg*

Right:
Stone piers carry the lattice-girder spans of Waterrow Viaduct on the Taunton–Barnstaple single line. A delicate-looking structure with timber deck and metal parapet railings, it was demolished for scrap after the line closed, though the stone piers still stand. Using angle-section plastic strip, a lattice-girder span can be a very satisfying model to build. *Gainsborough*

Top:
A more usual form of span for viaducts is plate steel as seen here at Crianlarich Viaduct on the West Highland line in 1914. The six spans carry cross members which support the trackbed. The spans are riveted together and rest on stone piers. *Real Photographs*

Above:
The London & South Western Railway's viaduct at Meldon in Devon is unusual in being two single-line viaducts with their latticework piers interlaced. It was built as single track in 1874 and doubled five years later. The arrangement can be clearly seen in this 1963 view. The viaduct is 550ft long and 150ft high. *R. C. Riley*

WAITING SHELTERS

THE designs of waiting shelters at stations and halts were as many and varied as the stations for which they were built. Though hundreds have succumbed to demolition with station closures and rationalisations which reduced stations to just one platform, a few survive. In addition, since the 1960s BR has added a whole range of new shelter designs at unstaffed and staffed stations, beginning with the awful steel-framed glass bus shelter and progressing to more enlightening and attractive structures.

Above:
The most delightful example of John Fowler's designs for the Oxford, Worcester & Wolverhampton Railway survived at Chipping Campden until the station closed in 1966. Divided into two rooms, the structure was built of shiplapped timber with a sloping roof concealed behind deep timber valancing. The two doorways were, latterly at least, without doors.
Author's collection

Left:
Similar to the little station buildings on the adjacent Wrington Vale Light Railway, this is the waiting room at Congresbury station in Somerset. Ship-lapped timber construction is employed under a tiled roof and with a sturdy brick chimney for the all-important waiting room fire (few waiting shelters boasted such refinements). The little bay window sets off a structure which deserves to be modelled.
Author's collection

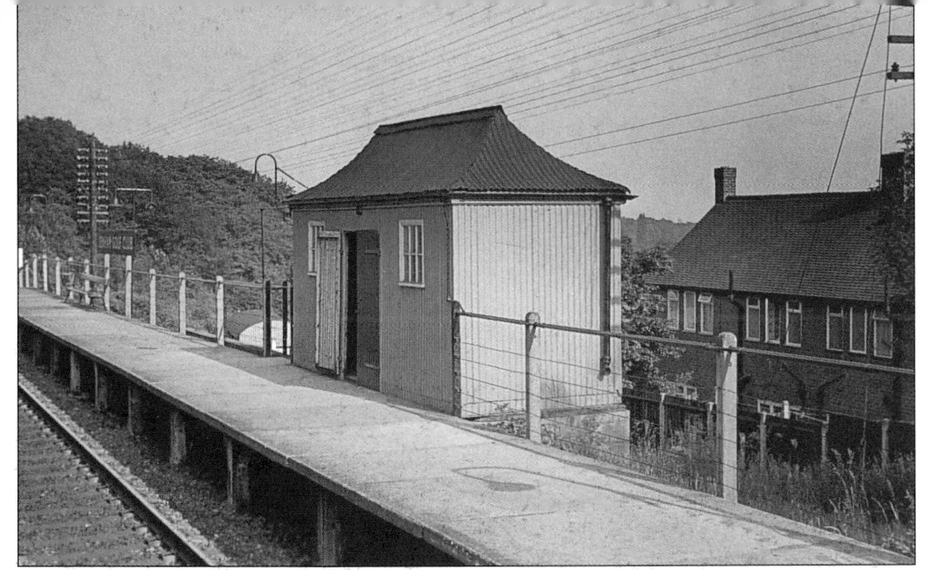

Left:
The 'pagoda'-roofed corrugated-iron sheds supplied to the GWR by Joseph Ash & Sons of Birmingham found widespread use as waiting shelters on stations and halts. It is doubtful if they were really intended for such use. Some examples, as here at Denham Golf Club, were equipped with double doors and two front windows. Many of those used as shelters had just a door opening and no windows. A wooden bench was provided inside, but seldom any lighting. *C. Totty*

Above:
The familiar style of wooden waiting shelter found at smaller Southern stations is represented here by Datchet, seen in the 1980s after a repaint. This timber-framed building had two small rooms (here with windows boarded over) and a recessed waiting area with seats. The sloping, felted roof formed a canopy with decorative timber valancing. This shelter was demolished in 1994. *Author*

Left:
The timber-framed LSWR waiting room at Virginia Water, seen in the 1960s when the base of a replacement shelter was under construction alongside. The external cladding is featheredged boarding, with a decorative valance around the top, which may once have been a canopy. The seat is a standard LSWR bench. *Author*

Right:
Once the private waiting room of the Marquis of Ailesbury, this red brick building was situated on the southbound platform of Savernake High Level station built by the Midland & South Western Junction Railway. It was similar in style to the MSWJR building at Cricklade, having a grey slate roof and a canopy supported on two cast-iron pillars. *Author's collection*

Left:
Another private waiting room, this time for Lord Lansdowne's Bowood House near Calne. His Lordship had the 'timber shed' built for £55 and it remained in his ownership until 1952 when BR took it over and named it Black Dog halt (see **Station Buildings, Western Region**). The structure was built against the stone retaining wall and was framed in timber and faced with shiplapped pitch-pine planks. The roof was slated and the wall at the Calne end was built of red bricks.
Don Lovelock

Right:
This small brick waiting room design matched the GWR red-brick stations of the 1898 design, with its blue-brick plinth and hipped slate roof. This example was at Colnbrook but there were numerous others which were similar. The small canopy has standard-pattern timber valancing and there is a handsome chimney stack.
Author's collection

Above:
Caythorpe on the Grantham–Lincoln section of the Great Northern Railway had a little timber waiting room clad in tongue-and-groove vertical boarding. The valancing around the top adds a nice detail touch, and this building has doors and a waiting room fire. *Ian Allan Library*

Below:
There is little clue as to where this structure might be, but it is so fine that I could not omit it. In this brick and timber building there would appear to be separate men's and women's waiting rooms plus toilets. The detail of the timber front is exceptional, with toplight windows, exposed framing and the tongue-and-groove boarded panels arranged in chevron pattern. *Ron Prattley*

Left:
The Bedford–Bletchley section of the LNWR Oxford–Cambridge line remains open and boasts an array of waiting shelters varying from original to modern. The shelter at Millbrook, seen here in 1994, is one of the originals, clad in tongue-and-groove vertical planks, and with a decorative valance around the top. Inside is a crude bench seat. *Author*

Right:
Moving on to more modern structures, this is the new Garston station in 1966 — actually a halt but the word was out of use by this time. The shelter is timber-framed and clad in corrugated iron — surely waiting-shelter design had reached rock bottom. *BR*

Left:
Looking modern and infinitely superior to the Garston shelter, Hadley Wood was older, having been rebuilt in the late 1950s/early 1960s with the quadrupling of this section of the East Coast main line. The shelter is steel and glass with weather screens and seats. *BR*

Right:
The nadir of the waiting shelter came in the 1960s when stations were destaffed and solid old buildings were replaced with these monstrosities, the dreaded 'bus shelters'. Hundreds of these steel and glass buildings were put up and many remain in use after 30 years. This example is at Oulton Broad North and was photographed in 1994. Subject to vandalism, they are often covered in graffiti or have their glass broken. *Author*

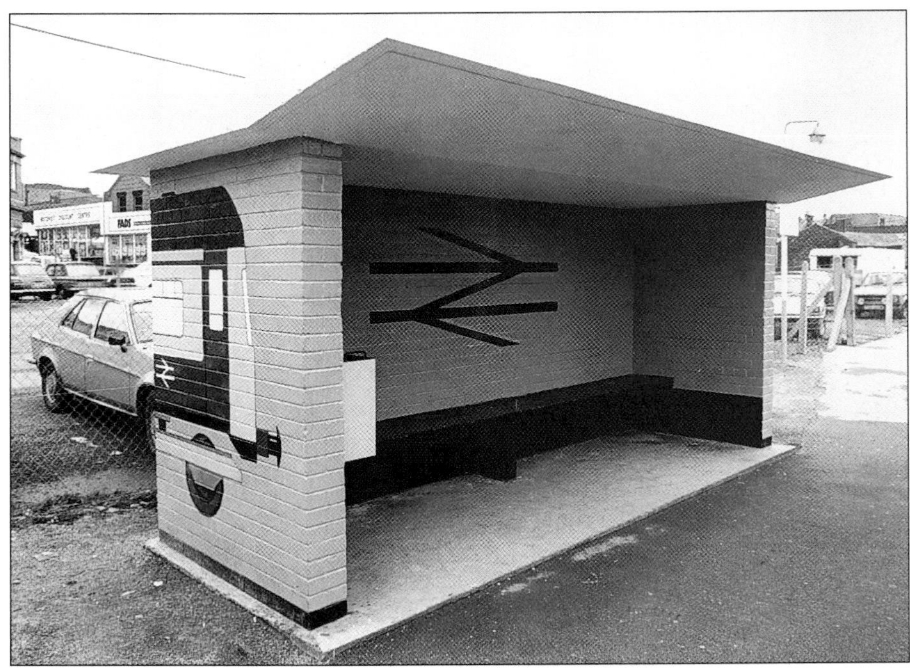

Left:
The need for vandal-resistant waiting shelters led to some varied solutions. At Wrexham Central this brick shelter has a reinforced concrete roof and a very solid bench seat. There's nothing to break and if you're inclined to decorate walls, well, BR has done it for you. Nevertheless, a potentially interesting subject for a layout set in the 1970s. *BR*

Right:
Penarth was one of 46 South Wales stations to receive improvements in the 1970s and this is its vandal-proof waiting shelter, new in 1975. Again, there is nothing to break, and apart from graffiti on the imitation-stone walls there is little damage which idle hands could do. *BR*

Above:
A brand-new 1980s station at Saltaire in West Yorkshire shows how solid traditional railway design has returned. This stone waiting shelter with stone-capped gables and slate roof is design to complement local architecture. Note, too, that Midland-Railway-style platform fencing has been used. *BR*

Below:
A range of steel-framed structures of ultra-modern industrial design have been introduced by BR at NSE and Regional stations in recent years. This waiting shelter at Lowestoft is one of the larger structures, its peaked roof being supported on four round columns. Draught screens and seats are provided. A smaller round-topped shelter is also used at some locations. *Author*

WATER COLUMNS

THE water column, essential for replenishing locomotives at depots and at stations *en route*, was a utilitarian device, yet strangely distinctive to the individual railway companies. Here was a giant tap — similar in concept to the modern mixer tap on a kitchen sink, and with just as much variety. The water column passed into history with the steam locomotive and it is unlikely that there are any left at all on BR. However, there is no shortage of them on the preserved steam railways, and there is a good variety, too.

Above:
The distinctive GWR water column seen at the platform end of Wiveliscombe station, although this could be almost any station on the system. The column has a straight arm with a flexible 'bag', a funnel into the drain, a grid on the platform below it, and a 'fire devil' to keep the frost away in winter. The hand-wheel valve can be clearly seen on its separate pedestal. Note the little flourish in the chocolate and cream paintwork — a common feature. *Author*

Left:
A GWR column in Southall motive power depot is a much more utilitarian example, with straight arm and column and a handle-operated valve. There's a concrete post to which the 'bag' can be tethered but no funnel and the drain is full of coal. A January 1965 view. *David Percival*

Above:
In the final days of Eastleigh steam depot, cleaners work on 'West Country' No 34024. The water column at this Southern depot has a sloping arm supported by a guy wire. There's a post to tether the bag, and a drain, but the 'fire devil' does not look as if it would be effective. The valve here has both a wheel valve and a 'T'-shaped stop cock key. *G. S. Cocks*

Below:
A column with cranked arm, handle-operated valve and no drain at an LMR depot in the last years of steam. *Ian Allan Library*

Right:
The driver fills his oil can on the 'fire devil' at an unidentified SR depot. The water column has no arm, just a turned-over top and a long flexible 'bag'. The wheel valve to turn on the supply is mounted on the column itself. The details of the drain can be readily seen.
S. C. Townroe

Below:
Cranked-arm London & North Eastern Railway water columns stand sentinel at Darlington station in 1966. The farther column has LNER and the date of manufacture, 1939, cast on it.
Ian Allan Library

Right:
This is the new design of standard water column introduced by BR in the 1950s. It was described as 'frost-proof' and it was said that it avoided waste of water. A wheel valve is fitted but no flexible 'bag'. *BR*

Below:
Lancashire & Yorkshire Railway columns stand at Mirfield depot in October 1966. These distinctive columns with their long flexible 'bags' each have their own gas lamp. The columns stand on a concrete base incorporating a drain and the separate wheel valve has its own column alongside. *L. A. Nixon*

Left:
Cranked-arm GNR columns and 'fire devils' at Doncaster motive power depot in January 1966. Three separate castings form the cranked arm.
L. A. Nixon

Right:
This distinctive column with its sloping cranked arm supported by a guy wire is a London, Brighton & South Coast Railway design, seen at Oxted in the 1950s.
C. R. L. Coles

Left:
An LMS 'Black Five' 4-6-0 takes water from the Highland Railway column at Helmsdale in September 1959. The Royal Mail coach is an ex-Highland Railway TPO, the last Highland coach in service. *Brian Stephenson*

WATER TANKS

WATER tanks were an essential feature at stations where locomotive supplies were needed in greater quantity than could be supplied from an adjacent main. They came in various sizes and both rectangular and round types were used.

Essential features were an operating valve, often a floating ball-valve arrangement, and a level indicator to show the depth of water. Some had an open top to collect rainwater and others were connected to a local supply, well or spring.

Above:
A rectangular tank by Ransomes & Rapier mounted on a brick base at Blenheim & Woodstock, a GWR branch terminus. This tank is fitted with its own outlet for filling a locomotive, operated by a pull chain. *J. Morss*

Below and top right:
The covered tank by Stothert & Pitt, engineers of Bath, at Savernake High Level station. The supply here was pumped up to the tank, which still remained intact in 1992. There must have been a long 'bag' from that outlet pipe when it was in use. The device with a little wheel is the depth indicator. The pump engine was housed under the tank. *Author*

Right:
A utilitarian riveted tank on a concrete frame served locomotives at Rolvenden on the Kent & East Sussex Light Railway.
Author's collection

Left:
Another survivor is this large covered tank at Kemble, supplied from a local spring. Kemble water was piped to Swindon through a trackside water main because it was ideal for locomotive use. This tank used to supply adjacent houses, too, and had a tall frame and 'header' tank mounted on top of it. In WR days it was painted chocolate and cream. *Author*

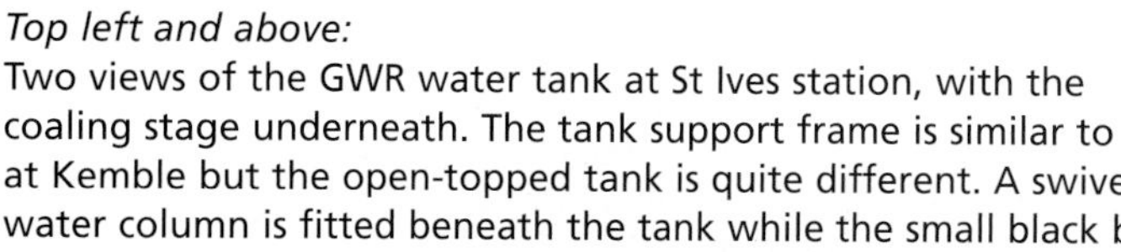

Top left and above:
Two views of the GWR water tank at St Ives station, with the coaling stage underneath. The tank support frame is similar to that at Kemble but the open-topped tank is quite different. A swivel water column is fitted beneath the tank while the small black ball on one end is the level indicator. *Author's collection*

Left:
Light railways tended to have fairly makeshift equipment. At Clevedon on the Weston, Clevedon & Portishead Light Railway in 1937 there stood this simple square tank on a stout timber frame. The feed pipe to the tank is clearly seen, as is the outlet with its long flexible 'bag'. A chain-pull operating system is employed. *Real Photographs*

Above:
There were several different versions of the familiar GWR conical water tank. These tanks were a storage tank and water column combined, and the pivoted filling arm can be seen to the right of the 'fire devil' with its very tall chimney. The depth indicator and chain-pull operating arm can be seen to the right of the tank. This tank stands on a tall column. There were shorter versions and also some tanks with a convex bottom rather than the flat version seen here at Ross-on-Wye. *E. T. Rawlins*

Left:
The former Witney passenger station of the Witney Railway became a goods depot when the line was extended to Fairford. This is the Witney Railway yard with its little covered water tank on a brick base in the foreground. The tank has acquired GWR livery in this view. *Real Photographs*

Above:
A simple round tank served the Kent & East Sussex Railway locomotives at Tenterden Town, where a Ford railbus is working the service in this 1930s view. The level indicator was a weight attached to a cable and looped over a pulley on the tank edge. Inside the tank the cable was attached to a float. Thus, when the tank was full, the float was at the top and the weight was low down the tank side. The weight can be clearly seen in this view, suggesting that there is not much water in the tank. *Real Photographs*

Left:
This fine cylindrical tank, of riveted construction, was photographed at an unrecorded London Midland Region station. It features a swivel arm and 'bag' with just a simple brazier to keep it from freezing. The tank has an open top with an access ladder and a couple of planks laid across the top. *BR*

WATER TROUGHS

Below:
A good view of Wiske Moor troughs on the East Coast main line near Northallerton, which shows the gulleys which served for drainage and also protected the ballast from being washed away. *I. S. Carr*

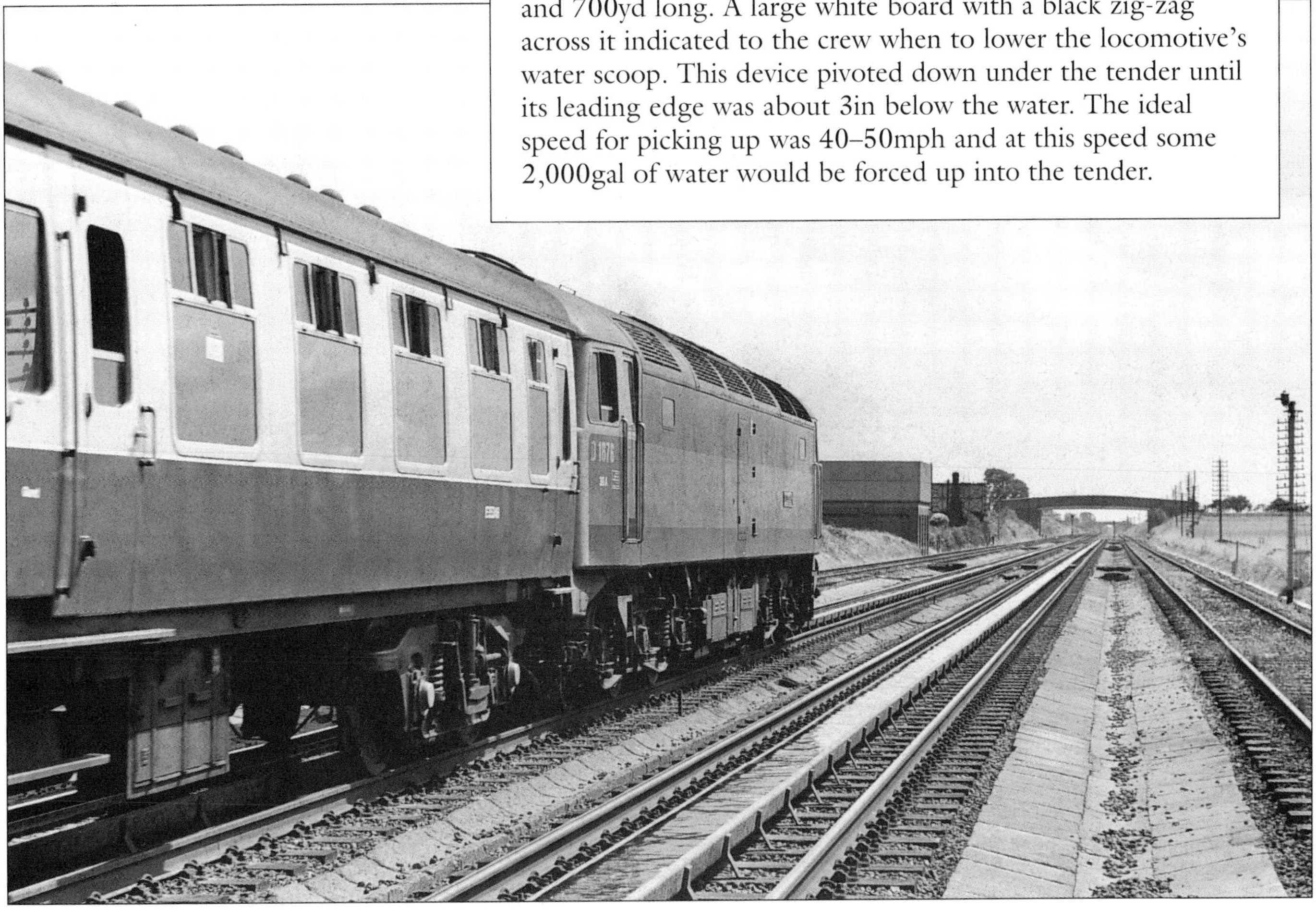

WATER troughs, which enabled locomotives to replenish their tenders without stopping, were invented by John Ramsbottom, the Chief Mechanical Engineer of the London & North Western Railway in the early years of the 20th century. At the height of steam operations there were troughs at 159 different sites in the UK, on the main lines of most major railways except those which formed the Southern Railway, where large-capacity tenders were used instead.

The troughs were 15in wide, 8in deep and between 500yd and 700yd long. A large white board with a black zig-zag across it indicated to the crew when to lower the locomotive's water scoop. This device pivoted down under the tender until its leading edge was about 3in below the water. The ideal speed for picking up was 40–50mph and at this speed some 2,000gal of water would be forced up into the tender.

Right:
Exminster water troughs, near Starcross, Devon, on the Great Western Railway. The storage tank acted like a giant cistern and had a valve arrangement which automatically filled the troughs after each use. The top edges of the troughs are turned inwards to reduce spillage.
Real Photographs

Right:
Some diesel locomotives were equipped to collect water to replenish train-heating boilers, as demonstrated here by an English Electric Type 4 diesel-electric on Dillicar troughs in 1964. Boards and slabs protect the ballast from being washed away by the overspill. *Eric Treacy*

Above:
Welded rails are being off-loaded at Strawfranks troughs, near Carstairs on the Scottish Region. The trough sections are fitted to brackets mounted on alternate sleepers. At the far end, it can be seen that the trough bottom slopes upwards to contain the water, there being no stop-end on the troughs. *BR*

Below:
Accumulations of locomotive ashes and ballast in the bottom of the troughs could cause serious damage. On a Sunday in June 1948 staff are cleaning Goring troughs on the Western Region. *F. H. Dillistone*

Above:
The warning board which indicated the commencement of water troughs.
Ian Allan Library

WEIGHBRIDGES

WEIGHING platforms were provided in most station goods yards to enable road vehicles to be weighed to ensure they were within legal load limits. The system usually consisted of a large cast-iron weighing table, linked underground to a calibrated instrument in a small adjacent office.

Left:
The smallest weighing table I have seen, photographed in 1992 at Stroud station, Gloucestershire. Now preserved on the station platform, it was used for weighing luggage barrows, the weight being indicated on the ornate cast-iron balance behind it. *Author*

Right:
The more usual goods yard weighbridge is seen here. This example at Handborough was supplied by H. Pooley & Son, which had the weighing machine contract for the GWR. The cast-iron weighing table is protected by an old rail, and the weight is indicated on equipment in the little office. An etched plate for the Pooley weighing table in 4mm scale is included in the Chris Leigh accessories range. *Author*

Below:
The weighbridge at Buntingford station on the Great Eastern Railway bears a strong resemblance to the standard GWR style. Though the offices varied in style, the basic arrangement was universal. *A. M. Lawrence*

Left:
The weighbridge, 1963 style. At Tyneside Central freight depot the then new arrangement provided a pair of weighbridges separated by the modern office building. On the right-hand weighing table is a Scammell 'mechanical horse', the usual BR local delivery vehicle of the period. In 4mm scale, models are available from Merit and Dapol. *BR*

List of Locations